ISSUES

The Opposite of Everything I Was Taught

Sue Roulusonis

DEDICATION

To everyone who's ever felt out of place and out of step with everyone else.
To those of you who were told you 'thought wrong' yet were still nagged by
the feeling that your way of thinking was not only right for you, but valid.
To those of you who've felt shut down and shut up.
If I can speak out, so can you.

CONTENTS

ACKNOWLEDGMENTS

There's no way I can acknowledge everyone here. I am fortunate to have so many wonderfully supportive people around me who put up with my shit. To those of you who've had to listen to my opinions, read every variation on my themes, listen to me whine about certain parts of the process, and are still willing to sit and have a drink with me after – you are my heroes.

1 JUST WORDS

Trump. God. Fuck. Chaos. Masturbate. Judgment.

Trump. God. Fuck. Chaos. Masturbate. Judgment.

If you heard me saying these words out loud, you'd have heard me almost sing them somewhat rhythmically. And if you were familiar with Kander and Ebb's musical Chicago, you might even hear a distinct similarity to the intro of their song, "The Cell Block Tango".

In this book, like in the song, each word is the subject of something explained later - all except the first word (I can't even bring myself to talk about that; I just threw that in for fun because it always gets a reaction).

By repeating those two lines, I have just accomplished three things:

First, I got your attention just by the words I chose to say.

Second, I minimized your reaction to them by repeating them.

Third, I changed your perception of them by associating them with a song. Even if the song wasn't familiar to you, just the association of those words with music altered your reception of them.

Do you know why?

Because they are *just words*, and they mean nothing.

We say that words have power, and they do - but they don't; words are stand-ins for thoughts and emotions, but they are not the thoughts and emotions themselves. If you think about the times that you've found yourself at a loss for words, you can understand what I'm saying. Words don't *have* meaning, they *convey* or carry meaning. There is a difference.

A sunrise can be beautiful, a person can be beautiful, and a song can be beautiful, and in each situation the word beautiful means something different. Beauty can be majestic, awe-inspiring, breath-taking, calming, intriguing, soothing – but those are just more words. Substitute one of those words for the word beautiful and you evoke a different thought – even though they can all mean beautiful. So you have a bunch of words that can all mean one thing, but be different on their own – although using them together can cause you to sound redundant.

Then there are the homonyms and homophones, the words that have more than one meaning and the words that sound the same that are spelled differently and mean something different, and it's the context in which they are used and the other words surrounding them that determine what that word conveys.

And then there are more words that have meanings that have changed over time or due to circumstance, expansive words that are used in situations that are less-than, and words that are names of things that became part of name-calling.

I could go on and on.

Is this fun word-play, or argumentative semantics?

Yes.

But what does it all mean?

It means nothing.

Until you decide everything it can mean.

We use words to persuade, bargain, plead, praise, encourage, denigrate, sing, and sometimes just to make noise. To sell rather than communicate. The funny thing about communication is that it doesn't need words; meaning can be shown by a look or action. An in-joke between two people with the same train of thought almost never has to be spoken; a look will be all that's necessary. Love and hate can be communicated through touch – a caress or a slap. A nod or a wink can mean agreement ... again, the list goes on.

Despite all this, we choose to elevate the power of the words themselves, because as stand-ins they are the short-hand method of selling something to more than one person at a time, like in a song, book, speech, or advertisement.

If we looked hard at the things we say, we would realize how very hypocritical we can be in our use of words with total disregard for their actual meanings, only occasionally striving to use them effectively rather than tactically. There are times we take care to use special, socially-acceptable buzzwords, tailoring speeches to each particular group of ears listening. Times we use words relative to our audiences with more intent to artfully deceive rather than to relate, with less concern of mutual communication and understanding and more just for the nodding agreement of the target audience (and maybe a few extra votes). Once we jump on pleasant-sounding words or word-sets we use them so often that they become trite and meaningless. Like in the child's game of Telephone, a word or phrase becomes mangled further down the line.

Our *United* States are divided on nearly every subject imaginable – bear in mind that our uniting together was in itself an act of separation. The meaning of *Love* is determined by the object of affection, calling for different behavior for each form, and *acts of love* are twisted into manipulative rules of obedience. There is talk of a God with *unlimited* power, but if that God is in a battle that he could potentially lose then his power is as unlimited as our cell phone data plans. Did the meaning change, or did our definition of it change? How well do we accept the words *thank you* if we know they are only said out of obligation?

Every so often when I'm listening to any form of media I'm reminded of Inigo Montoya from the movie "The Princess Bride" when he says, "You keep using that word. I do not think it means what you think it means."

Words are only as effective and as meaningful as the reader or listener deems them to be, because their meanings have become lost in our convoluted use of them. It's funny how we can give or take away the importance of words depending on what we are talking about or who we are talking to. Sometimes we only agree with things that may be said if the politically correct right words are used. Sometimes, we get so offended by the use of one word we ignore all of the others. We even vote for candidates who speak out of other's mouths (they don't all write their own speeches).

To take away the value and power of words, we overuse them or assign a different meaning in how they are used. One of the most common ways we play with that shows in our ability to disarm a derogatory title or phrase. A classic example is in the current use of the word *bitch*. This was once considered a powerful insult to women until we took over the word and made it our own. If I'm called a bitch, I'll just smile and say thank you.

You already know that words can mean nothing or everything; empty promises and declarations of love are examples you see every day. What this tells you is that you are always at a point of choice in accepting anything you are told. Anything. You can decide for yourself whether or not to believe anything by paying attention to more than just the words, including your own thoughts on the matter. Don't ever discount your own thoughts (as long as you know they are your own), because those are what serve you daily. Decisions you make always ultimately affect you the most. Listen to, read, or watch whatever you want, but do it with the awareness that you can choose how much you internalize. Be open to the fact that not everyone may have your best interests at heart, and even if they do they may not have what works for you.

And that includes what you find here. Consider that you have the Amazon rating option of everything; when you're done you answer the question "Was this helpful to you?" and know that whatever you answer is right.

You already *know*. Words are just words.

Fuck it.

2 THE TRUTH ABOUT THINKING FOR YOURSELF

Do you think for yourself? Do you know what your own Truth is?

I know this much is true:

All of it.

It's all true, every last bit of it. Your Truth ... my Truth. Even that guy sitting on the bus picking his teeth has his own Truth – and it's true.

What is truth?

Truth is what is real and accurate for a person. Our own truth is our beliefs based on how we feel about something. We learn what we believe and think by how we feel about something. Emotions are the biggest indicators of our own beliefs. A negative emotion shows us what is in discord with how we believe, and positive emotions reveal what resonates with us.

How do you know what your truths are or what you really think?

Now here is where it may get uncomfortable: check your gut, and ask: *why* is something your truth?

Most of us like to believe we actually think about things; but, if we were honest, we would realize that we live the majority of our lives out of habit and routine – as in, no thought required. What we think we 'think' about is more of a playback of repetition. It's like listening to music; we dance to the song we already know.

We are all in denial of how little we all truly think for ourselves by our outright refusal to believe that almost all of what we think we believe has been fed to us. Do many of us ever actually spend time questioning our beliefs on anything? Do we even know what we believe? Most of us aren't even aware of what we believe; we just go through our entire lives reacting to situations in ways we call 'normal' or 'common to us' without defining the reasons why. Then, we question our unhappiness or dissatisfaction later. To appease ourselves, we quote phrases like

If you do what you have always done, you will get what you have always gotten.

Of course, we only say things like that to people with *real* problems – because basic unhappiness or dissatisfaction is an accepted part of life, isn't it? *Life is hard. If it was easy, we wouldn't appreciate it. Nothing is perfect. If it seems too good to be true, it probably is.*

Bullshit. Math is hard to me, but it's not to a mathematician; appreciation and the value of anything is based on our perception of importance; perfection is in the eye of the beholder; and the idea of 'too good to be true' is another opinion based in fear.

I hate to break it to you, but the majority of what you believe on any subject at all was determined for you first by where you were born (this is also the most definitive proof on the existence of *collective consciousness*). You may resent the idea of and the word 'programming,' but you can't deny that your first beliefs on any subject came *from someone else*. What you feel about religion, marriage, sex, gender, education, politics, race, and any other hot-button topic, you *learned* the basics of in your hometown. *Children learn what they see* – and we were all children once. We were taught what everyone else around us was being taught, pretty much the same way, because there was little room/time/inclination to teach us to think for ourselves.

Think about this: the only times you found yourself thinking for yourself was when you *disagreed* with something you were told. Your following of, and agreement to, the establishment else was implicit, because it was *normal*.

But what was it that made you disagree? On the smaller, more personal scale, something inside of you stepped up and questioned the matter.

On the larger, more collective scale, when we want to point out someone else's wrong, disagreement with an idea gets boiled down to one phrase: "It's not normal."

Tell me, where did *your* normal come from?

You do realize that if you'd been born in a specific part of the world that you would have considered 9/11 to be a good day?

(The truth hurts, doesn't it?)

And then there are the over-thinkers; those of us who profess to studiously think about everything, justifying that overthinking is about getting a bigger picture of a situation, because it allows us to be fairer or make better decisions. One thing we refuse to acknowledge is that the trait of overthinking is almost always based in fear.

Don't think so?

(That was a gut reaction thought, wasn't it? Pay attention to that tidbit.)

Self-proclaimed overthinkers need to be able to judge the entire situation before we make any kind of decision. The proof that overthinking is fear-based is in the fact that most of the time the end answer we come up with *was our first thought*. Technically, we don't overthink to make sure we judge a situation fairly. We are looking for validation for that first thought or a pros and cons list in support of it.

I say 'most of the time' because sometimes we are able to glimpse a full picture without our normal filters; usually that reveals itself in an *Aha!* moment when something nudges us outside of the normal mental process we use – the one that usually prevents us from seeing another perspective.

We think we are covering all possible outcomes yet we actually filter more than we consider, because we are looking for validation for our answer *more than* the actual answer.

If you want to overthink something and be fair to include *all* possible variables, check your gut first. The gut reaction is immediate and emotional – emotional in that the response you come up with is always *felt*. That reaction shows you your belief, your truth, immediately. Right away, you *know* what you think.

Let's conduct a social experiment of sorts and talk about The Bible (yes, there may be a small element of interest in the idea of pushing buttons here). I'll start with two questions:

FIRST QUESTION: *which* Bible?

Now, why would I ask that? We all know which Bible I'm talking about, right?

Do we?

I could be talking about the *Hebrew Bible*, the *Shruti*, the *Tripitaka*, the *Akilattirattu Ammanai*, the *Talmud*, the *Dao de jing*, the *Analects of Confucius*, the *Qur'an*, the *Book of Mormon*, or many other religious texts.

Oh – you think I'm talking about *The Bible* bible?

Which version? With over 50 different translations, how do you know which one? The 73-book Catholic Bible, or the 66-book Christian Bible? The KJV? The NASV? The ASV? The NKJV? The NIV? The New World Translation?

Which Bible is yours and why?

(Are you beginning to get the picture here?)

SECOND QUESTION: *Are you willing to read anyone else's Bible?*

Why not? (I ask that because I *know* what the majority answer is.)

Because you know yours is the *true* Bible?

Who told you that?

13

Because you may have heard about one of their beliefs that you think is wrong and assume that everything else they believe is also wrong?

Are you *afraid* to read someone else's Bible for fear that you may be *tempted* to question your own beliefs?

(Am I the Devil for even suggesting that?)

Would reading something that you disagreed with make you shut the book before you finished it? Would you know why you disagreed?

Could you be open-minded enough to read it all the way through? Just to observe the thoughts of others?

What if you read something you *didn't* disagree with? Would that make you feel guilty? If it did, why? Would you feel you are betraying something? Or someone?

Have you been taught that it's wrong to question anything? Do you believe that it is? Or have you been taught that questioning an idea is only allowed if it has nothing to do with the religious beliefs you were brought up to adhere to? Remember, all scientific facts begin with a question of some kind. *Why? What if?* The true scientist allows for every possibility; he or she knows that you will always find proof of what you are looking for, but that the best way to prove a theory is by attempting to *dis-prove* it – an open mind is the absolute necessity. We accept and expect that, but we immediately shut down that idea when it comes to certain subjects. If your first reaction to the idea of reading outside of your faith is negative, you have just proved my point.

Reading the Bible of another faith is probably the easiest way to learn if you truly think for yourself, since most of our home-schooled beliefs have a basis in the religion of our region of birth. If your first reaction to that idea is negative, fearful, or even guilty, ask yourself why and be honest about the answer that comes to you. Then ask yourself why you came up with that answer.

Let's move on to positive thinking, because a positive mental attitude is one of the best motivators and a helpful pick-me-up. Do you consider yourself to be someone who has a positive mental attitude? Is it easy for you to think positively, or is your first reaction to anything new negative or hesitant? Are you 'trying' to be more positive? If it is 'work' to try to think positive, isn't that an admission that a positive attitude is going against the grain of what you actually believe? Where did you get such a negative attitude? Were you born with it? And, if you are working to think differently, isn't that another admission that you need to learn to un-learn the way you were *taught* to think?

Answer this again: were you taught *how* to think or *what* to think?

Is your head spinning yet?

Good. The best way to get out of old thinking patterns is usually by being jarred or surprised. The best comedians know this; by pointing out the extreme of a situation, they allow us the opportunity to give ourselves permission to look at things from a new perspective – and they make us happy to do so. And if we can't laugh at something they say (or if we get offended), we are made strikingly aware of our beliefs.

Each and every person has a singularly unique expression of who they are, despite basic similarities. The common denominator is the human factor. In that we are all the same. We all came from the same place, whether you believe God, Allah, Darwin, or none of the above. We started the same but live in different expressions of what is true for ourselves.

What is true for me may not be true for you. There is more than one way to skin a cat. There is also more than one way to make a soup, express emotion, write a song, paint a picture ... live a life.

Some writers swear by writing out their thoughts in pen and paper, other writers say they organize their thoughts better on a computer, and still others get inspired only when using a typewriter. A person can believe his or her life is worthless even while others see value and potential – but whose beliefs will that person rely on, ultimately, when they feel that a decision to live or die needs to be made? A jealous spouse can ruin a marriage even if his or her partner is faithful; a woman who believes her man is cheating or inclined to cheat will treat him with distrust – if she believes it; even if he's not cheating, it will still be true for her (and vice versa). Catholicism is divided on gender issues, yet all Catholics believe in the same God. Look at how many other religions there are, worshipping different Gods, with different rituals.

Our biggest problem is that we feel the need to impose what is true for us on others, as if it should be true for them, as well. We have decided that the beliefs which we swallowed should be forced down another's throat. We allow others their little 'opinions,' like favorite colors or foods, but assume we have the right to make their bigger decisions. We encourage "thinking outside of the box" in problem-solving. We are allowed to think outside of the box, but not live outside of the box? Where's the sense in this? At the same time, we resent those who try to force their truths on us.

Our allowances and tolerances for other's truths are incomplete; we only allow another person his or her own truth only so far. True allowance and tolerance needs to extend as far out as the possibility of something. Anything that can be thought of can be true. Anything that give us that inner feeling of "YES!" or "NO!" is what determines our truth, and our actions in accordance with it.

We act as if we are afraid to let people be themselves, thinking that harmony can only be achieved if we are all thinking, doing, and being the same. Then, we criticize schools for their standardized testing methods that supposedly judge intelligence and aptitude but don't account for differences in people. Then, we preach of Creators who would build a world of polarity but 'test' all of it the same.

Every coin has two sides, and it's the combination of both sides that make the coin. There is no coin if there is only one side; each side validates the existence of the other. Both sides are 'right.' All truths are true, because they are the basis for the actions of each individual.

Then again, thinking differently also depends on whether or not you want to. If you are happy, be happy. What I say and think or what anyone else says or thinks doesn't matter. Only what you think matters, because what you think directs your entire life.

However you believe we were created, we were created with differences, and we know what works best for us. Let your emotions guide you to your beliefs and see what you follow or react to. If you don't like something you find within, you can change it. Be only who you know you are, and not who you were told you should be. Search for the "YES!" in your soul; that is what is true - but allow others the same freedom.

Most importantly, make sure you are thinking for yourself. Your life will be better that way.

And that's the truth.

Think about it.

3 PERSPECTIVE

What is perspective? Perspective is a point of view. If you put a dot in the middle of a circle, you could stand anywhere on that circle and have a different view of the one dot. On the flip side of that same coin, if you stood on the dot and looked anywhere on the circle, even just a hair's turn would give you a different view of the circle.

Where you stand in relation to what you are perceiving is not the only factor that helps determine how you see it; your mental and physical health at the time, the people around you, the weather, and many other circumstances can cloud, alter, and/or block your view.

A Perspective with Pizza Rolls (A True Story):

You've just come home from work after a long day and your kid immediately hits you up
for a snack of pizza rolls the second you walk in the front door. While you know she is completely capable of waiting for you to put your bag down and take off your coat first, you know that the sooner you give her the pizza rolls, the sooner you can get to finally sit down *alone* with

the cup of coffee you plan to reheat from the full pot you didn't get a cup from in the morning when you rushed off to work. After you've put down your bag but before you even take off your jacket, you grab the bag of pizza rolls from the freezer, open the bag, dump a hearty amount on a plate and put it in the microwave. During the minute and a half they are 'cooking,' you take your jacket off and rush into your room to change out of your work clothes and bra and whip on the sweatpants and T-shirt you threw on the bed when you took them off in the morning. You rush back into the kitchen, grab a napkin, and head to the microwave and open the door just as the timer goes off. With one hand you let the plate of pizza rolls cool for a moment on the counter while you grab a mug and pour the morning's coffee into it and put that cup into the microwave with the other. While you're patting yourself on the back at your forethought to get the pizza rolls in the microwave before you were ready to reheat your coffee – economy of time is important, and you wouldn't have wanted to stand there and watch those damned pizza rolls 'cook' for a whole minute and a half before you could put that important cup of coffee in and watch that reheat for a whole minute – you realize that you are starving and grab a pizza roll off the plate you have them cooling on and shove it in your mouth, chewing fast because it's almost 'magic' time.

-- *Wait! That thing is fucking delicious!*

Let me try another one.

YUM!

With thirty seconds to go until your coffee is ready, you spend twenty seconds eating half of the delicious creations you were heating up for your kid and use the last ten to carry the plate to where your child is waiting in front of a video screen, throw it at her in the same manner a zoo employee would toss a steak at a lion, and offer up a prayer that what you left for her was enough to tide her over so you could enjoy your reheated coffee for a few quiet minutes. Your kid scarfs down the rest of the little filled dough-pillows you covet, seemingly content, and you finally get to enjoy your moment of quiet.

Two weeks later, you are home alone on a Friday night because the kid is at a sleepover. You are wearing your usual "I'm home" uniform, and you've already decided that even though tonight would be a perfect night to go out and try to have a life you either didn't have the money, gas, or motivation for it and chose to stay in. Because you're still a little on the fence about making the official decision *not* to go out, you have no idea what you want to do. You putz around for about a half hour before you decide on watching a movie; you spend another 20 minutes on deciding what you want to drink and whether or not it should be a grown-up drink (just because *you can*). It's another half hour gone before you decide on the movie and drink and you're finally sitting down in front of the TV – then you realize you forgot a snack. The night's indecisive theme hits you and before you play that 'what do I want?' game and waste any more time you decide to have some of those delicious pizza rolls. (After all, they only take a minute and a half to prepare.)

[One minute and a half later]

Okay. You are FINALLY ready to sit down and watch a movie with your drink and snack and – BONUS – it's only 10:30, so you still

21

have time to watch the whole movie before you go to bed. You take a first sip of wine, put the glass down on the coffee table next to you and pick up the plate of pizza rolls, pulling it close to your chest as you sink back into the couch while popping one in your mouth. The opening credits begin on your movie and

-- *What THE FUCK did I just put in my mouth???? Yuck, yuck, YUCK! These are disgusting!*

Immediately, you open your mouth to spit out the partially chewed, disgusting concoction of processed cheese, imitation tomato, and triple the amount of pretend meat back onto the plate, throw the plate down on the table in disgust, suck down half the glass of wine to get that terrible taste out of your mouth and slam that down, too. Then you grab the damn remote, shut the TV off, and head straight to bed, giving up.

They were the same pizza roles from the same Family Size bag that I opened two weeks earlier. What was it that made me enjoy them one night and hate them the other? I liked them that first day because I was starving, because I was pressed for time, because I had no motivation to entertain the thought of preparing a meal. I hated them the second time because there was none of the pressure, need, or rush that narrowed my focus – when you're hungry, almost anything will taste good. The night that I was taking time for myself my focus was on my own enjoyment, and the filters that work with personal preference were in charge. I wasn't starving, therefore my personal taste had more influence than my hunger. My perspective was different both of those nights because of the filters I was living through, and that made the difference in my reaction to the pizza rolls.

When we learn how to take pictures, we get a better understanding of perspectives. All of the elements that go into taking that perfect shot are perfect examples of methods used to predetermine and influence perspective. Giving this some thought can help you get an idea of your own perspectives and help you figure out if they are truly yours or if they were the direct result of an outside influence.

We understand the basics of taking pictures. When you take a picture, you focus the lens on your subject and snap the shutter button. Before the days of cell phone cameras and specialty filters, the photographer would have to position himself close to or away from his subject, depending on how wide he wanted the shot. He would have to use specialty lenses to zoom and change the focus, either color or black and white film, and he may need a separate flash bulb if one wasn't built into the camera. He would have to force a change in perspective to get the shot he wanted. Also back in those days, he would be limited on how many pictures he could take according to the capacity of his film roll. He would not have the option to see his picture until the roll of film was developed in his dark room.

With the digital cameras and cell phone cameras, the only limit to how many pictures a person can take is determined by the size of the device storage. Both have auto flash built in, the user can switch between black and white or color photos, and they have at least 20 filters that can be set before the picture is taken or used to alter the picture after it was taken.

This means that the lighting, distance from the subject, and even the subject itself doesn't matter as much as it used to. With the right color filter and lighting, a scene from a dump near a puddle can look like the beach, and vice versa. Social media photo applications can alter a person's appearance: an older woman can take her own picture first thing in the morning upon waking up, and within five minutes can have a self-portrait that looks like she took it after spending the morning fixing her hair and putting on makeup – ten years earlier.

These filters show every aspect of perspective. Zooming in on a subject - or cropping the 'bad stuff' out is a perspective in itself, showing whether or not you can see a 'big picture' or if your focus is too narrow. Color plays into mood, and the lighting determines how much is visible. There is also an irony to the analogy of letting others develop your photographs – what you see in your final picture can be determined by the quality of the business developing it for you.

We used to have to wait about two weeks for an outside service to develop our pictures. Those who have grown up with cell phone cameras will never understand the agony of waiting for their pictures to develop, paying a small fortune (like posting bail for your memories) only to get them back overexposed and ruined.

People who work in media are well aware of the valuable effects of filter and focus and use that to force a specific perspective on their audience. They determine what is seen by how close to the subject they are; they can hide imperfections in darker lighting, and their choices of color are either psychology-related or an advertising trick (let the color of the product being featured show up all through the print i.e., color association and imprinting).

The same can be said of a person speaking or writing. Different angles and slants on a story, combined with the tone used, can provide a desired viewpoint in the listener or reader. These are also examples of filters used to force perspective.

Another influence on our perspective is what we learned in our closest circles through repetition. Repetition is the core of learning anything. The more something is repeated, the more it will be internalized. A parent's opinion repeated daily over the years can imprint itself on a child. Classroom lectures, church sermons, newspapers and other news media outlets can shape the opinions and viewpoints of the listener, simply by repetition. The younger the listener is – the more captive the audience – the more can be 'transferred.'

These are just a few examples of how perspective can be derived from an outside source. Our own lives, our daily occurrences, can create filters from within. "Once bitten, twice shy." *This has happened to me before; I will be vigilante in not letting it happen again.* Awareness of a previous experience will color how you look at something similar – even if the circumstances and/or people involved are new. If we have had interaction with people who always seem to have a specific intention for some type of gain, we find it hard to believe that another person may not be working from a similar type of angle in their dealings with us. If our partner in a relationship has broken our trust, we find it hard to trust another partner.

Again, repetition is the core of learning anything. This does not only apply to what we consider to be negative. A person being treated with love will learn how to be loved and give love in return. The discussion here is primarily of the negative aspects of filters we can learn, because such filters can block an honest viewpoint and constrict perspective. Positive filters create open minds; negative filters close them off.

These learned filters, whatever their source, decrease the ability to think for oneself. A lot of personal stress is created, too, when a filtered viewpoint wars with an inner question of that perspective. If you have been taught that knowledge is best personified by a certain type like a teacher, a priest, or a wealthy person and a man comes up to you and tells you that the sky is blue – something you know and believe – but he is dressed like Elvis, talks like Elvis, and says he *is* Elvis, will you be able to believe him or listen to anything else he tells you, or will you discount him and what he says because he does not fit your perspective of knowledge? What if he says something to you that makes a lot of sense, yet makes you question something you believe in? Will you ignore what he says because of who he says he is, even if you feel with all your heart he is right?

Once you've questioned your own belief or knowledge of anything even momentarily, it will nag at you forever, and every time you find yourself acting on that perspective, you will question yourself. There is no bigger battle than the one you have with you. You may feel that by changing your mind you will have lost any ground you have established beneath you. You could possibly feel you are being disloyal to someone or betraying an idea. Yes, it may feel like agony at the time, but it is actually a wonderful thing, because knowing more about yourself will put you in a better position to make healthier decisions for yourself, decisions that might actually make you happier. Disagreeing with another person's perspective is not betrayal and has nothing to do with loyalty. It is also not a statement that another person is wrong; it just says that what is right for them might not be right for you.

You can think about perspectives as clothing; we should all be wearing what fits.

It is an incredibly freeing feeling when you release the burden of outside perspectives that don't fit you, especially when you realize how far into the smallest details of your life that they had influenced. When you understand you are truly making your own decisions you will be happier with yourself, even to the point of being a little proud. You will be more secure in your accomplishments, no matter how small, and you will feel less like a victim of 'life'.

In this respect, Cinderella got it right: wearing shoes that fit will make a difference.

4 GOING IN CIRCLES

If it seems that there are ideas repeated herein, it is because there are; nearly everything is connected. What starts out as a standalone idea or theme has common roots and connections underneath the layers with other ideas and themes. It is only the specific details added together in a unique combination that give anything or anyone its singular identity. Split the hairs down far enough, and it's just the one head that's left.

That idea of splitting hairs – arguing the small details, is pervasive in our world, but like most everything else we take it only halfway and use it when it's convenient for us and never in its full magnitude. We split hairs to define our differences and ignore the fact that those same arguments define our connectedness. Remember the idea of 'isolate and exclude'? The details we argue are the ones that point out specific differences to *deny or obscure* connectedness. The argument starts on the basis of connection; we split hairs to remove all traces of it, but the hairs we are splitting are the details we've added on our own in our identities, and *denial* of anything implies a need to prove that something is *not* true.

Like innocent until proven guilty, proof is needed to deny a *given truth*.

This may all sound rather circular – and it is. No matter where you start and where you go, you always end up with you.

Let's start with you, you who have the same spirit and essence of any other being on this planet. We are all born the same way. We are the same at our roots of being. The 'details' come in the form of your parents influence first: eye and hair color, physical build, and congenital traits. Adding to the mix are your parents' ages, social standing, income level, geographical location, talents, and ethnicity. On top of that are the feelings, emotions, and thoughts that they themselves have as a result of their environment that have been filtered through their own personal experiences. Your own individuality comes from your own innate qualities (we'll get into that a little later) and what happens to them when enmeshed with those of your parents' – whether encouraged, discouraged, or a little of both.

Remember, too, that your parents each started out the same way. Every birth is a brand new mix of details, but at the heart and soul are all 'just' human. So, one can argue that another is different because of hair color, but if you shave both their heads that detail is non-existent and they are the same.

Basically, the things that make us different from others are those details of circumstance that were added to our base states, and the 'splitting hairs' – the removal of them, brings us back to our basic sameness. It is the focus on them that creates separateness.

If we truly believed that God is all, and God is in everything, and all around us then we have to accept that God is in each one of us (making us the same), but expressed differently (the details that separate us).

I can sing a song and you can sing a song. You may be singing a church hymn and I may be singing a top 40 selection; both of them are songs no matter the difference in melody, tempo and lyrics, and despite the difference in song selection both of us are still singing.

Even our innate qualities don't fully separate us fully from the pack. These qualities I speak of are our talents and inner passions that we are born with. The inner ideas of self that reveal themselves first almost usually in some kind of discord – when we don't realize we have the same talent as someone else, or we hear or see something and *feel* a sense of 'that's not me'. Some of us are artists, empaths, musicians, and healers (and the list goes on); however, all of these seemingly separate qualities all have one base thing in common: they are the 'fixers', they bring things together in unity. They provide basically the same results, but use different methods of reaching them. When we focus on our differences we only notice the difference in how things are done, without acknowledging the outcome is always the same.

The only time we acknowledge sameness is when we have a set parameter or an idea of a norm for unity, and strongly encourage conforming to a list of societal 'shoulds'. We know innately that *united we stand*, but we don't seem to know that our standing together needs to be a voluntary choice for unity to be happy – and it *will* be, through acceptance of others. Instead, we think to shortcut the way to true unity with a formula or set of rules: dress alike, look alike, talk alike – we mistake *uniformity* for unity. What? We can't all be on the same team if we're not wearing the same shirts? (And in true circular fashion, the idea of uniformity does as much to exclude as it does to include.)

We do this everywhere: in business when an idea works it gets copied, movies begin to follow a formula – and how crazy is it that someone figured out a formula for a boy band? Instead of coming into a form of unity organically through our talents and passions, we force a uniform idea and expect others to adhere to it. But what happens then? The formula becomes overused, people become oversaturated with it (movies are insultingly called 'formulaic'), and everyone is dissatisfied until someone shows up with a new thought and then we rush to copy that. The new thought is praised for a little while, copied, and then becomes cliché. And the cycle continues.

Fashion is a great example of forced conformity. As a noun, *fashion* is defined in two ways:

- A popular trend, especially in styles of dress and ornamentation.
- A manner of behavior or doing something.

Fashion is also defined as a verb:

- To make into a particular or required form.

Can you see the irony here? Acceptable FASHION (n.) is only had after one has been properly FASHIONED (v.).

What is more fickle than fashion? Who wears the wigs and hose now? What decade did a woman have to live in to be beautiful as a size 14?

We strive to follow a fashion determined by others based on a new idea – but as soon as everybody is following it, the idea becomes old, foolish, and 'so last year'.

- until time has passed, and the look makes a comeback. Revere, kill, revive. The same old song you haven't heard in a while.

Are we sensing another pattern here? Another circle?

We do this with leaders and celebrities, too. We love to watch them rise, and love even more to watch them fall. Raise them up and then crucify them. What's funny is that we enjoy them for their differences and the newness it brings to us, but get tired of them once that fresh air becomes stale – which happens when we think to keep copying it.

How many times can you listen to the same song before you get sick of it?

Now think about how you feel about that song when you hear it for the first time in 20 years; it's new all over again and you get reminded of why you loved it once before. Sort of like how we revere someone we've crucified after they died.

Yet even this silly merry-go-round we ride reveals a truth in that we really do appreciate what's different.

But we don't, right?

We say that there's more than one way to skin a cat, yet rush to point out when someone is 'doing it wrong'. We know that it is the combination of different ingredients that make a steak tasty but deny that differences of opinion, preference and nature can lead to a fulfilling life. We appreciate the differing (and even discordant) sounds of each instrument coming together to make a beautiful symphony, but don't even consider that different people can live together in harmony.

All this running around in circles we do. We say that the journey matters more than the destination but tell each other to keep our eyes on the prize. Yes, having a focus on direction can keep us moving, but that prize isn't necessarily what we really want; it is only a means to an end - a step on a continuous journey. Think about it: once you've achieved a goal, do you just stop? No. You set a new goal. Most of us barely rest a few minutes and enjoy the accomplishment of achievement before we rush to get to the next step. The achievement of a goal is not the end of the game but merely a step along the way. The prize of a good job is not the job, but what the job affords us in lifestyle, and the lifestyle we have is what we believe determines our personal level of happiness. Our goals all have to do with being or attaining that which we believe will make us happy and satisfied, and human nature is never satisfied because there is always more to get.

This is not a matter of selfishness – at least, not the idea of selfishness that we take to be a negative trait. Moving onto the next goal is part of general progress, evolution ... *life*. Life is a series of experiences, and we move from one to another every single day.

It's all about the movement, the journey. No matter how many goals we achieve or only come close to achieving, what we look at at the end is not the achievement itself but everything that happened along the way. The journey.

We all have our own yellow brick road to follow. It starts with our dissatisfaction with where or what we are; our first steps are in a small but widening circle, spiraling outward, as if we don't yet know which way to go. We meet people along the way, those that guide us, befriend us, teach us, confuse us, and mislead us. Some of the situations we find ourselves in are happy, magical, and peaceful; others are scary and threatening. Ultimately we reach what we think is the end, only to realize we are back where we started, and what we went looking for was already with us.

We also realize the necessity of that journey – after the fact, in many cases. When we are too close to be able to see what is in front of us we need a measure of distance to view the whole picture. The obstacles we encounter along the way are there to provide necessary contrast, to question, enhance, or destroy previously-held ideas, and allow us to see without filters – sort of like taking someone for granted, then realizing their value to you later after you have had close interactions with someone who has taken advantage of you. Hindsight is still a clearer vision. We either appreciate what we have or we get taught how to.

We never do really reach an end at all - unless you consider death to be an end – because the end of one thing is always the beginning of another as long as there is movement. When you complete a grade of school or reach a goal, you move onto the next. Even when you overcome an obstacle or achieve a goal, you move onto the next – and, arguably, everything can be perceived as an obstacle of some kind; we just decide for ourselves whether or not it actually gets in the way and to what degree it restricts or influences your movement. Do you dread your morning alarm? Is getting up in the morning a problem? You can't start your day without getting up, can you? So, by getting up in the morning despite the hardship of the rude awakening of the alarm at that ungodly hour, you have already overcome one obstacle. High school education requirements comprise a process that can be perceived as an obstacle to graduation; job interviews are the hurdles (obstacles) to jobs; childhood is an inescapable obstacle to adulthood – you have to get through one to get to the other. Even the attainment of a goal is an obstacle to the next, because you usually don't see more of what you want until you get what you want.

Circles. Our mistakes begin by assuming there is a direct path to everything, and that only one way is the way. How many of us were told that we could not succeed in life without a college degree? How many people are employed in jobs that have nothing to do with their degree - while paying the cost of that degree for the rest of their lives? How many people dropped out of college to create big corporations? That belief about college being the be-all and end-all has created a shortage of people who work in specialty trades. Follow the money? You can be the biggest CEO of the world's largest corporation – but it will still suck if there's no one around to fix the air conditioning in your windowed corner office in July. Pretty soon, our HVAC technicians could be commanding the same hourly rate as lawyers –

that is, until the trade schools become more societally desirable than universities and the pendulum gets forced in another direction.

This is not a tirade against education; it's a means of pointing out that there are many ways to learn, and having the "I Was There" badge does not guarantee anything.

The idea of one direct path to anything is laughable, because there are too many other variables to consider, like the movement of people and situations around you. You can give yourself a path as basic as a schooling plan: by such-and-such year you will graduate college – but what happens if you or a family member gets sick and schooling is delayed? Car accidents, major injuries, war, terrorist attacks, financial issues, clinical depression, unplanned pregnancies, and even fear can force alterations on that course. Despite the best planning, your control of a journey only extends as far as you personally, and your journey will always intersect with the journeys of others who you cannot control. You are not here alone.

The launch of a spacecraft is carefully planned, but with gravity and planetary movements and everything else that is going on in space, course corrections are expected – and required - and still missions are successful.

That is life; a journey of course corrections in zig-zags, curves, hills and valleys. But that is the best part. If life worked in a straight line there would be no *life* to it. Nobody likes being in a rut, and that's exactly what is created by continually walking in a straight line.

We have to learn to embrace that circle, and it will embrace us. When you flat-line, you are dead. Without the lows in life, we wouldn't appreciate the highs; if everyone around us was the same, life would have no flavor.

And still, no matter where you start or how you end, you are still left with just you. Your own 'completion' depends entirely on you and how you navigate the journey, but you always end up back where you started, with you.

Maybe it would be easier to think of the Circle of Life as the Circles of Life – and then think of all those circles as bubbles. Since there's no angry way to say bubbles, it can lighten up what we think about life in general.

All throughout this book there are numerous comments and thoughts of seemingly the same things, and some of them may appear quite ridiculous or extreme. Showing one example of an idea shows its relation to one train of thought or one aspect of life; showing more than one can convey the scope of it – how far it really goes and how many areas it reaches. Like everything else, one idea ripples outward. Every subject in this book is interconnected with every other subject included, because if there is a truth in anything it is a universal Truth and not a situational truth, no matter how many hairs we try to split.

5 LABELS

I have been socially and societally filed under many different labels: my age categorizes me as Generation X, my color has supposedly put me at the front of the bus, but my gender moves me back a few seats.

My job-title labels made it easy for some to sort my status and worth. Pity the poor fool who works in any service industry. (There is an awareness of this widespread subcategorization in the statement that you can judge others by 'how they treat their waiter'.)

I am labeled – and therefore judged - by my color, my job, my age, my looks, my choices, my hobbies, my lifestyle, my political status, my religious beliefs, my clothing, my children, my friends, my pets, the color of my nail polish, and many other divisive (and derisive) categories, but none more than for my lack of a certain body part.

When I was a kid, my label was 'just a girl' and with that came many assumptions about what I was allowed and not allowed to do or be.

When I got married I was someone else's possession, mirror, representative, daycare provider, secretary. *Mrs. Not-Me.*

After I gave birth, I was just a mother (with the included presumed loss of sexuality points).

When my label changed to Divorcee, I was judged as an adulteress – because a girl would never leave her man unless she had another lined up. Moving into new neighborhood as a single mother, I was labelled a cougar and MILF – because as 'just a girl' I couldn't possibly want to be alone for long.

As a female over the age of 35 but under 60, I'm a lost demographic to the marketing world, with only a place as a prop (if I still look young enough to be a method of pre-screening for Viagra).

Because I'm a girl, when I'm angry I'm 'on the rag'. If I'm hurt, I'm overreacting. When I have an opinion, I'm bossy. When I say no, I am a bitch (but if I say yes I'm a slut). When I'm assertive, I'm masculine (or trying to be).

I have this to say about penis envy: *while there may be times I wish I had one, it may not be in the manner you assume.*

This is not about sexism, even if it does seem that way; I can only speak with authority of the labels I've dealt with the most – and this just goes to show how many of our societal thoughts and practices are interconnected.

There is nothing more exclusionary or belittling than living under someone else's labels. Our society has managed to take the art of labeling to its zenith, using them not just as methods of organization but as a base for determining inclusion and exclusion. We have a collective need to label people and things - to put them in specific categories to determine value, worth, and thus our treatment of them. White or black, gay or straight, male or female, Christian or Heathen, Republican or Democrat, liberal or conservative, shy or outgoing, etc., we have this need to separate; you are either this or that. Further subdivisions are only for purposes of further exclusion.

As a country, the only thing we stand united on are those labels we use to isolate and exclude. First, there's Us and Them: our nation versus every other nation. Then we break down the Us and Them to our government versus our people, labeling the government as Them, the source of blame for all of our unhappiness, excluding ourselves as cogs from the machine that put them there by our support through our tolerance and our ideas of perpetuating 'normal' and 'standard'. Then, the Us and Them labels are used between individuals – and then we really begin to break it down. The wonderful idea of there being a Me and You with the ability to come together and create something wonderful *because* of our differences becomes a perverted idea that unity only comes out of uniformity, and if You are not the same as Me, you are out; that's where the labels come in.

In treating people according to labels, we deny not only the beauty of their own uniqueness but our own as well, and our connection to them. Try as you may, you cannot deny our connectedness; it has already been established that we all bleed the same way.

This is all part of our general hypocrisy of using acceptance and denial interchangeably. I am unique, but you are different.

Labels aren't always bad. Being part of a group is like being part of a club or church with the privilege of enjoying fellowship with people with whom you have something in common. We have ethnic histories we like to preserve, too. It is possible to be proud of our individual lineage, gender, and traits and still be aware of and celebrate our connectedness with others. In that respect labels are a means of inclusion.

Yet even that idea of inclusion holds a measure of exclusion. Segregation is an example of both inclusion and exclusion, in deference to perceived statuses. Look at the use of labels in consumerism and how we value them; nobody knows the value of the label better than teenagers who go out of their way to wear the right ones (as if having the label emblazoned on the shoulder, chest, or across the ass deems inclusion).

We do have to be careful how we judge that behavior, because they did learn that somewhere. We also have to look at how we perpetuate it with our own preoccupation with and consideration of labels.

I have spent my life trying to fight past the labels I have been given, yet I see my child needing to have a label to feel a sense of belonging. Labels aren't good or bad, they are good *and* bad – it's all in what we do with them.

Labelling different spices ensures that cinnamon will not be put in a tomato sauce. You don't want to put unleaded gas in a diesel engine, therefore different fuels need to be labelled. You will want to know if one of your dinner guests is a vegetarian so you don't try to serve him a steak. Makeup is made for people of every color.

Labels on things are good for definition of a thing; the difference between labelling a thing and a person is that a label on a person is not the entire definition, it only defines one aspect or trait. No human is of a singular definition. When we use our labels as blanket definitions of people, we diminish everything else about them and lessen their value as people.

None of the labels I wear define all of me – not even my name; I'm not the only Susan in this world, and my full name at birth was my mother's full name as well. Calling a blue marker a blue marker is inadequate because it doesn't cover all the shades of blue. Everybody is a little bit of something else. Masculine and feminine aren't even all-encompassing words; we all have the ability to be both.

The idea of the stereotype comes out of labelling people. Unfortunately, we follow our tendency of taking ideas too far or not far enough, and even a stereotypical label is not a full definition; even the classic stereotypes can have differences or traits that vary by degree. How would you define a feminist? A child?

I am not this or that; I am this *and* that. We are all this and that. We are different and the same *at the same time.* Pointing out differences in others also points out what is different about you to those others, and you are opening up yourself for judgment in return.

The only labels that really mean anything are the ones you put on your underwear for summer camp.

6 WE ARE ALL IDIOTS

You are an idiot.

Yes, I'm talking to you. Does it bother you that I would say that? Actually, it shouldn't, because I don't even know you – and you know that. How can I be an authority on who you are and how dare I think to be if we've never met? Does seeing those words in black and white make a difference – make it real? You read those words on paper, you were not able to see the look on my face when I said them and you could not hear my tone of voice, either – which makes them just *words.*

Sticks and stones...?

For the record, I'm an idiot, too.

I already told you that I love to play with words, purposely choosing those that might get more of a reaction or overusing some to take any sting away. Sometimes, I will use a word twice in one sentence and mean it differently each time. Even if it seems I'm not, I'm quite deliberate with words. (Wordplay is a bit of a turn-on for me.)

Usually when we call someone an idiot, we are speaking derogatorily at them and putting them down. I am not using the term 'idiot' as a description of people who have an actual lack of capacity to learn. That is cruel. My basic definition is that the idiot is the person who unknowingly acts in a self-sabotaging manner counterproductive to his or her own goals. The person who shoots herself in the foot. The conventional use of the word in conversation is from a place of judgment; we use it to mock people, to keep them down when they've made a mistake, to discourage them from doing something we don't want them to do, and to insult them for daring to think differently than we do. It implies ignorance, whether deliberate or not (regarding ignorance, keep in mind that there is such a thing as honest ignorance; none of us know everything, and that's not a bad thing).

Idiot is one of the words that I have appropriated into my personal vocabulary, giving it my own definition and a different level of power – which effectively removes the sting from its use, whether I am using it or it is being used against me.

Words used to hurt me. A lot. I grew up with name-calling, body-shaming, limiting words, and those that conveyed consistent disapproval and disappointment. Because I believed them, I was an idiot. I grew up to be a living translation of those same words I heard as a child – and when I heard them later, they were coming from my own head and in my own voice. That made me a bigger idiot. Not only did I give someone else the authority to tell me who I was, I began to repeat those words to myself in my own, loathing self-talk.

I didn't know. Ergo; idiot.

First, I had to learn that the words from others directed at me or about me had nothing to do with who I was. Their words were spoken from their own perspective; they were not thinking the way I was with the awareness, experience or knowledge that I have – they were only speaking from their own. *Not mine.*

After that bit of understanding – and it's only a bit; I still have to keep reminding myself of that – I had to start paying attention to how I talked to myself. I had to decide which of their words were true, false, or just words and then watch which ones I chose to repeat. I had to learn not to be an idiot about it.

Idiots are ignorant; they don't *know.*

'Ignorant' is another funny word. Ignorance is a lack of knowledge, yet when we call someone ignorant we are implying deliberate denial of something. We say racists are ignorant because they do know about acceptance and tolerance, but they are refusing to acknowledge it.

On the other hand, we say that ignorance is bliss – usually when we are talking about a child's ability to be happy because she doesn't know how many things are 'out there' that could make her unhappy. So, a person can be in a position of truly not knowing or knowing-but-denying.

Either way, that person is an idiot.

We have a tendency to think less of another person (or ourselves) for not knowing something. Why is that? None of us were born knowing everything, and what we do know we learned on the way – and everyone's journey is different, having started at different places and taking different turns and loops.

As kids, we delighted in learning new things and never thought less of ourselves for not knowing – until adults decided to lord their 'knowledge' over us and used knowing vs. not knowing as a measure on a scorecard. *You ignorant idiot.* How dare you not know? How dare you *think* you know?

We have to learn to learn better. We have to go back to the time when learning (and having to learn) was a good thing. When learning was a part of exploring life and not the verbal regurgitation of someone else's words.

The bottom line is none of us know everything and because there will always be something we don't know, we will always be ignorant of that thing – which makes us all idiots, technically.

I have accepted that I am an idiot, but now after all I've learned *so far*, the word is different to me. When a friend does something silly, I call them an idiot. When I trip and fall, I call myself an idiot while I laugh. My personal use of the word with affection and towards people I am affectionate with has changed my connotation behind the word – it even changes its meaning during my occasional nasty self-talk.

It's easy to forget that words used in self-talk have even more power than when they come from other sources. If we begin to know that we are the authority on who we are, we need to learn to be *especially* careful with how we talk to ourselves – or, we have to change the meaning behind the word so that if we can't get out of the habit of using it we've dulled the blade so it won't hurt (or as much).

I regularly call myself an idiot. When I stub my toe, spill my coffee, or make any mistake I call myself an idiot, stupid idiot, or fucking idiot – depending on the degree of the mistake. Either way, I'm an idiot. But things have changed; because of my use of the word with affection and with affection behind it the sting has lessened. I smile now when I call someone or myself an idiot. You'd be surprised at what a difference it makes.

Go back to the idea of labels and see the way we use them to mock, isolate, include, and exclude. Labels are just words. Words are merely stand-ins for ideas and never fully convey a meaning; we do know this because we are taught to pay attention to context, tone, and body-language: the *word supporters*. Their ineffectiveness in conveying a meaning can also be attributed to the person hearing the words and whether or not they understand them or are able to understand them through their own life-experience-filters and perceived meanings. In some cases, it is or is almost like dealing with a language barrier.

A touch or a glance can convey the idea of love better than the phrase "I love you" does. There are moments when we thrill at hearing those words, and at other times we've said that those words were not enough. Which is it? Is it a good thing or a bad thing to say "I love you"?

It's okay to be an idiot; it's okay not to know something – there's no shame in it. We learn by experience or out of the desire for experience. Even knowing something doesn't mean you know everything about a subject, either. A person who does not wear a bra would not understand the complaint made about what bras do to the shoulders. You can have a medical degree and still not know all there is to know about medicine. Different legal matters require different specialties of law. A person considered to be an authority on a subject may know the most, but not everything.

Knowing everything means there is nothing more to learn, to do, to see, or to be. We've already determined that life is a journey, and the journey is through the unknown.

And as long as there are things we don't know, we are idiots. Accept it. Embrace the idea; it only means you have so much more to look forward   to   –   and   so   much   less   to   fear.

7 A VILLAGE OF IDIOTS

In the continuing vein of wordplay and the deliberate use of both meanings of a word, I have more to say about us idiots; in particular, the idiots we are raising.

For fun, let's call them *kidiots*.

As a reminder, let's go back to my functional general definition: "the person who unknowingly acts in a self-sabotaging manner counterproductive to his or her own goals. The person who shoots herself in the foot. The conventional use of the word in conversation is from a place of judgment; we use it to mock people, to keep them down when they've made a mistake, to discourage them from doing something we don't want them to do, and to insult them for daring to think differently than we do."

The key to taking the bullet out of that particular gun is, again, in the actual definition of the word. The person who shoots himself in the foot does not do it deliberately. The idiot does not realize the consequences of his actions. He does not know, and he does not know that he does not know. He is basically a child, or child-like.

And we, as a people, think that mocking children for their ignorance is the way to help them figure things out.

Society's children, those of the 'next' generation (regardless of the generation you belong to) are typically derided simply for being children, for being ignorant (uninformed) … for being idiots. The timeless phrase that begins with, "When I was a child …" is the most common example. It is used in such a way to tell the new generation that our problems and our lives were always worse than anything they might be going through now. They are idiots because they don't appreciate that they have more than we did, or how easy they have it by comparison.

Actually, that makes us idiots – because we are the ones who don't know. Why? Because what we went through with the generation before is different than what our children are going through with us; we are ignorant of their struggles.

My parents are idiots. Of course, I'm speaking as a spawn of their generation, those Baby Boomers. (I'm part of Generation X now, and we have to deal with those idiot Generation Y-ers and Millennials.)

I watched how they raised me, and I can tell you firsthand that they did pretty much everything wrong. Through all of my adolescent criticism of them, there was one thing that stuck out to me: they didn't know they were wrong. I got the traditional When-I-Was-A-Child lectures from my father, too, so I decided to look at his father, as well.

What I see is that the kidiots spawned of every generation are looked at as a group who have no idea what the fuck they are doing. My father didn't agree with all of his father's parenting methods and tried to change them – just as I am doing with my own children. Children across history have taken the seeds of what they've learned and created a garden that was different from the gardens of their childhood. Then they interact and get together with others who've landscaped their lives differently, and they share seeds with each other.

What that means first is that our generation's children have been raised differently than we were. The newer technology, sociology, prejudices, living standards, and flowers and weeds have created a new environment – and while we may have been the ones to create it, we don't have the first idea of what it's like to live in it, like our children do. Who knows what allergic reactions they may have to our flowers?

I have only had to walk through metal detectors at airports and government buildings and nowhere else when I was younger. Whether we think about it consciously or not, there is an awareness of the reason they are necessary and that behind-the-scenes knowledge can have an effect on our general thoughts and actions in those areas.

I have never had to walk through a metal detector just to get into school. *School.* Imagine starting the day like that? You don't think that would affect a general mindset? We did not have that influence, that mindset. Our children that do, our idiots, have it differently.

Of course, it's their fault. They are the ones who listen to that stupid music, spend all of their time in front of those stupid video screens and worship those stupid reality (reality?) celebrities, and allow themselves to be influenced by them.

Like it or not, those weeds came from our gardens. We insult our society's children for buying what we sold them. They wouldn't have opportunity to enjoy those violent movies and violent video games if it weren't for us idiots who created them. Look at the selection we have laid before them.

Yes, we. Unless your child has been raised in a bubble, with only you for influence and guidance, you are not the sole 'parent' to that child, and how you parent your own children has an impact on every other child with which yours comes into contact. Each and every one of us, with our own gardens, plays a role in the influence of our collective group of children – even those of us who don't have any, because we are part of the society around them. Our participation in society, in whatever capacity, impacts the newer generation. We are a collective of individual landscapers who raised them, and we are the adults who teach them at school, who maintain certain norms, the babysitters, the inventors, the money-makers, who give example to them when they see how we interact with them and others.

As the society around them, we are their parents, the landscapers of their village.

We warn children of the 'monkey see, monkey do' mentality and forget that we are also what the monkeys are looking at. They watch us when we cut their parents off in traffic, give good or poor customer service, and let doors slam in their faces. They watch their parents' reactions to these events, as well. And they will watch how their parents treat you when they bump into you on the street, when they are demanding service, or when they go through the 10-items-or-less line in the supermarket with a full cart – and then take in your reaction.

When they begin to go out alone and in small groups they will notice how you may watch them. They will notice your coming to a conclusion about their worth by your perusal of their color, gender, hairstyles, and clothing. They will see your distrust of them while they are walking through the aisles in a store. They will notice your dismissal of them when you don't show them the same deference you would show an adult. They will hear the change in the tone of your voice when you speak to them – if you deign to speak to them.

We know how our village raised us, but we don't know how our own village is raising younger generations, and we are ignorant of the consequences of that upbringing.

If we are going to condemn our generation's spawn as a collective, then we need to own up to our being part of the village that is raising them.

We are both the idiot elders of one village and the kidiots of another; it doesn't matter how old you are.

Remember when Elvis was a threat? When children ran away to join the circus?

It doesn't matter which side of the fence you were on; you were still an idiot, weren't you?

The denial of this vicious circle highlights the hypocrisy in all of it.

We pretend to recognize that when children are born they are the most pure, loving, honest, and open – the most godlike. They are born wise, they love unconditionally, and they think for themselves. Then we squash that all out of them by forcing them to *grow up*. What we encouraged in them as small children we began to discourage them when they got older. Midway to middle age they become conflicted trying to reconcile what they see with what they know. We tell them they need to leave the child behind and become an adult. What we are really telling them is that they need to conform, to follow, to adhere to the dictates of whatever society is in power. We ridicule the child as being young and stupid, and manipulate them into following a norm. They are forced to make a choice: grow up or suffer the consequences that those of us who drank the Kool-aid will unleash on them (hell, we can't be miserable alone).

The height of hypocrisy is what happens when we ourselves get older: we berate ourselves for losing that inner child. We learn that we stopped playing, stopped enjoying the little things. A part of us becomes sad, and we want to be children again. We now envy the children we were just ridiculing.

This is usually when the so-called 'midlife crisis' occurs. The man that we poke fun at for chasing younger women in the obvious effort to be younger and the woman who believes plastic surgery is the key to youth; the spouse who realizes his or her life has just become a matter of settling, not really living, and wants out of the marriage; the person who realizes he or she got this far and is still not happy. Then, there are the underachievers among us who feel we got this far and haven't the perspective to see what was already in us, what we were born with, and how valid that was.

This is almost a mirror conflict of what we went through as children, and again we have to make a choice to settle or rebel. The settlers sit back with the fatalistic attitude of "It is what it is, I'll just have to make the best of it" – which will only make them slightly happier. Some of them won't even try for that; their 'acceptance' makes them more miserable each passing year, but they stick to their guns about their inability to change anything. The rebellious ones leave 20 year careers behind, taking leaps of faith to follow their dreams; they go back to school; they start trying new things; they begin trying to follow their hearts because they realize that is what it takes to be happy – and they realize their happiness matters. They become childlike again, and try to become what they wanted to be when they grew up (back when they were children and knew what that was).

Of course, they are scoffed at for acting like children.

This happens generation after generation. Children are wonderful, then they aren't, and then they are. We learn on our own how we were taught to leave the child behind to grow up, only to grow up and want to be that child again, yet we still don't do anything to try to skip that particular loop.

If we remember what it was like for us as kidiots, we might learn a little sympathy for what the new ones are going through. If we were as wise as we give ourselves credit for, we would not criticize them for being who they are but we would take responsibility for what we tried to mold them into and celebrate their rebellious desire to think for themselves.

Maybe one day we can look at them and say lovingly, "What idiots!" and fondly smile in the remembrance of the time that we, too, held those same thoughts, tried the same things and kept shooting ourselves in the foot. Maybe one day, we will appreciate the journey they are going through from the perspective of those who have done the same thing and grown from the experience, allowing them the same growth opportunity, without mockery. Who knows what that will teach them? What if what they try, works? Wouldn't that make you feel more secure about your own future as a senior citizen, when the kidiots are old enough to start affecting what our benefits will be?

My own parents know that I think they are idiots, but they also know that I don't question their love towards me and that I understand that they were doing the best they could *with what they knew*. Ignorance doesn't make people wrong, it just means they are unaware; true idiocy is not deliberate. I saw the changes my parents tried to make to break away from their perceived idiocy of their own parents. I began to see and realize more about them when I became a parent myself and tried to do things my way, the way I thought my parents should have done with me – and I got firsthand experience of how well or how badly that turned out. When I realize that I might have been wrong in my assessments, I go out of my way to call them and tell them that I was the idiot. I was unaware of many of their reasons for doing things they did or thinking the things they thought until I experienced similar circumstances myself

One of the biggest continuous arguments my father and I would enjoy together was about his fear-based parenting method. The 'would you rather be feared or respected' debate was a constant one of ours. When my older daughter was a teenager, she put me through the ringer (to put it mildly). I remember on one particularly frustrating day

I called my father. I said to him, "I still disagree with your way of fear-based parenting – but right now I understand why you used it!"

The bottom line is that we are responsible for thinking for ourselves, and paying attention to whether or not we are truly thinking for ourselves or just regurgitating what we swallowed. To do that we have to pay attention to what we *don't* know as much as what we do know. This will remove our ignorance of the part we play in the whole and the impact we have on the collective.

The jury is still out on how well I helped raise my own children. If anything, I hope that they understand that I raised them with the love and knowledge I knew at the time and that even if I still made mistakes, they saw a conscious effort on my part to make sure that they were new mistakes made out of ignorance and not repeated ones. I will be completely happy if one day they are able to look back while thinking of me and say affectionately, "She was an idiot."

But remember, if we stop being idiots we can stop raising them.

8 LEARNING TO WALK

Learning to walk is the greatest life metaphor. Stand up, take baby steps, practice, fall down, get back up again, go, run. We have created and preached so many different variations of this metaphor - and the only time we actually meant it to its fullest definition was when we physically taught a child to walk.

Teaching our children to walk is the only thing we have actually taught them directly and purely – separate from our beliefs and prejudices, with actual honest support and enthusiasm. It is also the only time we do not judge them for being children.

Let's relive the experience: The baby that has been lying down since the beginning of his or her life, dependent on others for physical support and getting from here to there, is now attempting to do these actions on his own. She begins to consciously and deliberately roll over, with each new movement showing her what she is beginning to have control over. His newly discovered arm strength allows him to push his body upward from the floor or bed, and he realizes how much more he is able to see with the new vantage point. She sees something she wants to touch across the room and tries to reach for it with her arms. When he realizes he isn't close enough, he might grab something and pull himself in that direction. Then, she becomes aware that while her arms can pull her legs can push. Pulling with his arms and pushing with his legs becomes the crawl. Eventually, she will try to do what everyone else around her is doing, and she will try to stand up.

At this point, we (his parents, family members, and friends) are watching closely and getting excited about the world that is opening up for him. We are taking pictures, praising her and cheering her on. The first time he stands on his own is an Event and celebrated. She starts taking steps, and we encourage her to hold onto solid objects around her for support – we even offer our hands. When he tries to walk without support, we move things out of his way that could hurt him, and we keep ourselves within his reach. All the while, we are singing her praises, letting her know that we believe in her, encouraging her to keep trying. He falls down, and we comfort him and tell him that it's okay and help him get back up again. She falls down again; this time we let her figure out how to get back up by herself, but we let her know that if she has trouble that we will help her. The first few steps he takes on his own are immortalized in film and shared with the world around us. *Behold the child, taking his first steps!*

And then, once they learn to walk, they are on their own. *Honey, I can't carry you; you are too heavy. No, son, you don't need to be carried; you can walk.*

After the child learns to walk, everything else he learns is by observing and modelling us and learning how to follow 'the rules.' Our focus becomes less and less on them as individual, special beings as we incorporate 'the rest of our lives' into our time schedules, and their lives begin to seep into the category of *obligation*. We used to drop everything to grab the camera to record their 'firsts,' but everything after that is old hat and not newsworthy. First lost tooth, first real potty accomplishment, first word (even first swear), first award, first visit with Santa … we show them that the firsts are the most important and that what comes after that is … well, *secondary*.

That is what they learn happens with them, too. *I'll get to you later, after I finish with work. Try to get a ride to soccer practice; I have a meeting. Honey, I have responsibilities.*

Each passing day, our time with them is filled with less enthusiasm and more of a sense of responsibility. This is not what we want, or what we want to happen. We don't plan it. We do still love and enjoy them, but real life seeps in. Now, we have to TEACH them about the world and its rules. We have to prepare them for What Is Coming Next.

What *is* coming next? Responsibility? Obligations? Hurt? Disappointment? Pain?

We send the child to daycare, preschool, and school, where specific rules are introduced and enforced. The originality they displayed as babies and new beings – that was once celebrated –now needs to be suppressed or stifled by set rules of conformity and societal norms. The excitement we showed at their signs of interest and exploration in anything has been tempered by the direction we feel we need to face them towards; *You need to learn this first; there will be time later for the things you are interested in.* They are taught the same way to be the same.

Like we were.

When they get older and try to 'walk' in different directions, we are no longer there for them – not as honestly as we were the first time. Now, we judge them for what they want to do and criticize them for how they go about it. We let our filters and beliefs decide our enthusiasm and support levels. *You want to be like Hulk Hogan? Honey, you know wrestling is fake, right? You aren't as big as he is and won't be as strong. You should focus on something you can use your brain for. Do you know how many others want to be like him? Do you really think you have a chance?* We 'teach' them conditions. *You need to make money first (you need money to make money). He didn't get where he is without connections. Do something reasonable first, then work your way up to that in your free time.* If we don't appreciate wrestling, we even teach them – by our actions, tone of voice, facial expressions, and (sometimes) direct words – that what they want to do or be is stupid. Actually, we fear they might embarrass us.

Then we tell them things we don't really mean: *You can be anything you want. Be yourself. If you want to go for something, put your heart into it.* Of course, we don't mean it. They have to follow certain rules, they can't be too different, and they have real-life, important things that need to take up their time and attention first. They need to be realistic.

And we expect them to believe what we say? How, when we talk out of both sides of our mouths?

Even the basic schooling they are required to have has been proven to be misleading, omissive, altered, prejudiced, oppressive, and in some cases just wrong. Yet they are still being taught the same way the generations before them were. We teach them who their heroes should be by searching out those who made the most impact on society – people who accomplished what they did by ignoring the rules. We teach that those "heroes" who broke the rules are wonderful, but that our children can't possibly be wonderful because they aren't allowed to break the rules?

Thomas Edison said he failed at inventing the light bulb over 10,000 times, and he is considered one of the greatest inventors. We teach our kids that failure is 'kind of okay', but if you fail more than once you should give it up and try doing something else – something more reasonable. Three strikes you're out, right?

Thomas Edison's passion and focus showed us that it doesn't matter how many times you fall; you can still get up and succeed.

He showed us the proverbial light, and yet we are still in the dark. We teach our children that passion, focus and interest has a limit or a 'failure cap;' what they learn is that they are not worthy to be another Thomas Edison.

But, by all means celebrate the rule-breakers. The other ones, anyway.

The children now are still learning to walk, in the metaphorical sense, but instead of the parental support, encouragement and happy enthusiasm they received from us when they were taking their first physical steps, we shoot them in the foot. *Walk NOW, kid!* We judge them for being too young to know who they are and how they feel about anything. We remind them that they are not Thomas Edison and that failure is an indication that it is time to quit. We make sure they are aware of all the odds against them (and we do that constantly). We tell them what they think and how they think is wrong. If they do try to make a difference or change the score, we patronize them, telling them they are doing it wrong.

What if that was how we taught them to physically walk? Imagine this scenario:

The child is just starting to sit up and falls over. We laugh and sneer at his stupidity and youth. *Look what he thinks he can do!* When she is taking her first steps she falls down for the first time; we help her back up, but now we are unsure if she should try again and our hesitancy shows (we may even suggest she stay down). He tries to walk after falling once (despite our warnings); when he starts to wobble he reaches for our supportive hand, but we are not offering it as readily because we are not sure if he's doing the right thing – and he falls again. Now, we help him up but tell him he may have made a mistake in trying to walk. She wants to try again; we've decided she's on her own. Instead of encouraging him to try again, we say things like: *Are you sure you want to do that again? Look what happened last time. Maybe you should wait until you are bigger and smarter.* We get worse, too: *I don't believe you can do it; you've fallen twice already. I can't believe you are foolish enough to try again!*

How many of us would have learned to walk under those conditions?

Over the years, children have tried to take stands against what they perceive to be injustices. We insult their perception because it is not our own and attempt to take away their voices by telling them they aren't old enough to have one.

Teach them to walk, then shoot them in the foot.

The best example is the most current:

This generation's children are taking the shooting a little more literally, in their schools. They are trying to make changes and taking their first steps towards stopping this pattern of behavior that seems to be increasing alarmingly. They are standing up, standing together, and speaking out. They are trying to bring attention to the both the problem and its components.

They are attempting to do what the country is trying to do about terrorism: acknowledge and identify the problem and take measures to prevent further terrorist attacks. They are doing the same thing on a smaller scale that we as a country are doing on a larger scale: trying to disarm their attackers.

They have two strikes against them right off the bat: they are *kids*, and their fight is with the inner establishment and big business.

They would have more support if they were battling another country. These children are essentially challenging their parents, and we won't have that, will we?

Because we said so.

We play the age card: *What could you know? You're a kid.* Even their supporters aren't all totally supportive. *Nice try, kid, but it's not enough. You're doing it wrong.* Or, we discount the good they are trying to do by comparing it to the bad or stupid they did.

I read a social media post from a peer regarding a television interview with some survivors of the school shooting in Parkland, FL. While he did first say they made some good points and had some valid arguments, he negated his support immediately; a student declared that they were the generation that had to live with school shootings, and his response was both patronizing and demoralizing by mentioning that their generation had no business attempting to dictate national policy because they "are not smart enough to not eat the soap [re: Tide Pods]"

You'll have to try to walk on your own. I've seen you fall; I'm not going to help an idiot. But, good luck, kid.

(None of us in the older generations ever did anything stupid, did we?)

We allow our politicians and leaders to denigrate them with name-calling and age-shaming.

(Is it necessary to mention here that our behavior towards the children in this situation is the same behavior we 'train' them to not do?)

When do we begin to understand that 'the norm' is not always right, and that the only way of trying to make it right is to go against it? We say we understand this idea, yet try to squash those that actually attempt it – *because* they are going against the norm. Which is it? Do we really want to make things better? If we don't think things are good now, obviously things have to change. How can we manage to create change if we try to keep everything the same?

If any of us sat back and thought about our own childhood, what would we discover? Did we have issues with our parents, our churches, our schools, or our government? Has anything changed? Did we change anything? Did we even try? If we tried to change anything, how well were our attempts received? How did we feel about how we were treated?

We all remember what that felt like, even if we deny it now – and we *are* denying it, otherwise our attitudes towards youth would be different now. Do we resent or fear children so much that we force them to endure what we went through and call it a rite of passage? To what end? To keep it all the same?

Our children (and the children of every generation) are a microcosm of the country. We can see the obvious parallels in high school cliques and hierarchies. What they've learned from our larger collective is what we've taught them in word and deed. They are our mirrors, reflecting back to us what we have been doing; ergo, their methods of rebellion are our own.

Technically, we should be flattered by their imitation, but we can't be until we admit that the idiots in the village have been raised by idiots.

It is not up to them to earn our respect. Respect is a mutual idea; it can be given but it can never be forced. To receive it, one must be willing to give it.

What is the point in teaching children to walk if we really don't want them to?

9 PROOF OF LOVE

We have this notion embedded in our stories and minds that love is a thing to be proven, like some kind of scientific theory. While the chemistry of love – or, rather, basic sexual attraction – is something that can be measured physiologically, the emotional, feeling side cannot. In actuality, it doesn't need to be, because it is always, *always*, visible.

Ovid said, "Love, and a cough, are not concealed."

It is human nature to lean towards things we enjoy, are interested in … *love*. We live between two general ideas of love and fear – not *hate*, hate is a by-product of fear (we don't fear what we hate; we hate what we fear). Our motivation is the drive for love – the happiness we want to achieve from being able to do what we love and/or being with whom we love. Whether our actual intention is to move towards love or it is to move away from fear, the direction is the same.

When we love something, or even just *enjoy* it, it shows. It shows in our faces, our attitudes, the amount of attention we give it, and for how long it can hold our attention. Why do we have hobbies?

What accounts for our 'special interests'? We join online communities/support groups to connect with others who have the same interests; we tattoo the brand of our favorite motorcycle on our skin; we devote time and money – our two 'precious' commodities – towards what we enjoy … what we *love*.

We do the same with people. We desire to spend the most time with or around those we enjoy/like/love the most. Our actions reflect our preferences. We invest time and thought in them. *It shows*. Our actions follow our focus of attention. Always.

Remember, *actions speak louder than words*.

Now, here, it is necessary to point out the difference between two very separate ideas that are almost always linked – incorrectly – together:

"Actions speak louder than words" and *"If you love me, you will* ___ "

The first is the result of love; the second is the conditional manipulation of another's love. Two very different pieces of fruit.

We know what love feels like. We know what we love, and we know what it feels to be loved. Even the person who considers him or herself the most unloved has at least one solid idea – *even if* that person feels that the only being that has shown him or her love was 'only' a pet. It is still love, and love is love is love.

You know when someone loves you because you can *feel* it. If you can't, here are a few possible reasons why:

1. The obvious: that person *doesn't* love you.

2. Unreasonable expectation: Love isn't conditional; our desire for 'proof' often stems from our *expectations* of another - and any

sort of expectation is unreasonable because we will never fully know the degree of another's motivation towards love/away from fear. We ignore that we have expectations of another when they 'follow through' – but even that is the result of their core motivation.

Another aspect of unreasonable expectation comes from our lack of knowledge of the other person. We often expect another to show their love the same way that we would, and we miss when they are showing love the way they know. You could be sitting on his couch expecting him to sit and spend time with you, but instead, he is outside washing your car, putting special effort into scrubbing the tire rims – you expect him to spend time *with* you, and he is spending his time *for* you. Is his love less because it is expressed differently than yours? When *you* love someone, you *know* them; you know what they value, and you would know if they value you.

3. Lack of trust: Here is a bit of a sticky wicket. There could be a lack of trust in another because they have hurt you in some way. The reason for their hurting you could be the simple fact that they don't love you, or because they were following their own lines of impulses/compulsions/motivations – which, in some cases, is *not* a reflection of the measure of their love but a reaction to that inner motivation. There may be degrees of love – of *preference* - but in certain situations that preference is more an aversion to what is feared as opposed to choosing what is loved (the lesser of two evils; making a value judgment choice between what will hurt and what will hurt *less*). This is obvious in the person who doesn't trust the idea of love; he or she has been hurt before and, in the expectation of being hurt again,

will either keep a noticeable distance or will hurt their significant other 'first' (as in, *before* they can be hurt). Some may even continue hurting their partner in small ways as a means of 'testing' their love needing to find some proof or guarantee that it will continue.

There is also the possibility that your lack of trust in another person has *nothing* to do with that other person and has *everything* to do with your own feelings of unworthiness. You might feel that you don't believe in love, but if you look closer you will realize that you don't believe someone could love you. Remember, when you say you don't trust one thing, you are showing absolute trust in its opposite. If your reasons for a lack of trust stem from a feeling of lack in yourself, you will end up putting unreasonable expectations on the other person, forcing them to perform Herculean tasks in a vain attempt to prove something to you that you will never see unless you first believe it could even exist. Then, too, if they don't express love in the way you expect them to – because they don't show it the way *you* do – you still won't see it.

Forcing someone to prove love to you will never fill any lack you feel in yourself, either. Two individuals come together as one unit, but separate parts of the foundation. If either or both are flawed, the foundation will not be stable. One bad day could topple it all.

Know yourself. Love yourself. *First.* Then you will be able to know and love another.

You never, ever, need proof of love from another person. If you think you do, you may want to take a good, hard look at things. Real love is involuntary and unconditional. Think about every single one of your preferences of any kind; you really can't pinpoint the *one* reason for your fascination or interest – it may always be a mix of consistent themes, traits or attributes, but there is always *one* unknown aspect that solidifies your 'connection.'

There is a common definition of 'unconditional' that many people live by regarding those they love: they love the other *in spite* of how they are treated by them.

That definition is incomplete, though.

Unconditional means 'without condition, unqualified, unrestricted' – as in *no expectations.*

Yes, it is possible to believe you love someone even if they treat you badly, however, if you expect anything from them, you are not giving love unconditionally. How many times have you heard someone else (or even yourself) say something like, "After all I did for him/her, you'd think that he/she would [fill in the blank]." That type of statement verifies that fact that anything done for the other person was done with some idea of expected gain or response – and that only serves to prove that people seem to believe they can *make* someone love them.

As basic human beings, treating each other with kindness should be automatic. Kindness is a form of love. We do tend to treat our favorites with a little more deference and special attention, however, we are not to assume that what we do for them should be rewarded. Love acts out of love, without need or expectation of gain or recognition.

I'll be the first to admit that I have gotten pretty pissed off at the person I held a door for who didn't thank me for it – I've even sarcastically yelled, "You're welcome!" after them (once or twice) – and then one day I realized that I was the jackass, not them. I did not hold the door for them to receive credit for it, so why was I expecting it? I hold the door open for another person because I feel it is the right thing to do. Knowing what it is like to have a door slammed in my face makes me want to prevent another from having to deal with it, especially if I can prevent it. I hold the door open for others out of respect and kindness, and any time I do something like that I feel good.

It feels good to do good.

If that's the case, I have already been rewarded for my kindness; why, then, should I expect double payment in the form of a thank you? And why should I feel slighted if I don't receive it? Does my forcing you to acknowledge my kindness provide me with anything of value? We've all seen children scolded by their parents into saying 'Thank you' for a gift or kindness, and we are well aware that they are only following orders or fulfilling an obligation. Is that the kind of 'love' we want to receive from another?

Real love – real, unconditional love - wants what is best for the other person – actually, what *they think* is best for them. *I love you and I support you in your decision to be who you are, to follow your own path, to make your own choices – even if those preferences are not my own because I want you to be happy. That* is love without condition. If the other person is feeling that same love, the two of them will find that what they both want is decidedly similar, and no 'sacrifices' need to be made.

It is often said that relationships take work. Once we call participation in anything 'work,' we take away from what it really is, and we begin looking for some form of payment for fulfilling our duties. We talk of compromise, even though we know the definition of the word means to settle or to accept lower than desirable standards. What business does that have with love? When you do something out of love, you never feel like it's a compromise; you do it because you *want* to. If that means you are taking less than you may have initially wanted, you are not settling for less, you are making a choice based on what you value, what is important to you. We make choices like that all the time; but when they are made in a relationship, why do we consider it work and expect something in return?

We are willing to pay more for an item we want, and we have our own reasons for wanting a specific brand, flavor, color, texture, etc. When we make the purchase, we turn over our money without a second thought, because we know we are trading the money for something we want – we make a value judgment. When I make a purchase that I am happy with, I have never once gone back to the store and complained that another store sold a similar item for less, because I got the one I wanted exactly when I wanted it.

If you think you have the right to force someone to prove *anything* to you, you may want to question *your own* 'love.' Why do you need to receive something from another? What are you missing on your own? Validation? You will never get that fully from another person because that is not where it comes from. Do you think of love as a means for *gain*?

Don't *ever* let yourselves be manipulated into doing *anything* to 'prove' your love, and don't attempt to use that same form of coercion on another. No person who truly loves you will ever think to force you into anything. If *you* are doing the forcing, you may need to check your mirror. How are you showing love by pushing your preference on another? By attempting to take away their own choice? Love should never resemble a prison.

We are not supposed to try and make anyone happy, either. *Trying* implies work, and work is *not* love-based motivation. When we are 'working' at love, our motivation is based out of a fear of losing it. We could never do everything the exact way someone else would want it or expect it because we don't walk in his or her exact shoes. We don't *know*.

When we do *know*, it is easy because our actions and reactions are in sync with theirs in shared energy and vibration. It is not 'work;' it is a natural partnership, harmonious orchestration. Two individuals bringing their best selves to each other, but *for* their own selves.

It starts with *you*.

Love isn't work; it doesn't need 'proof.' It just *is*.

Be the love you wish to see, and you will feel it without having to look for proof of it.

10 SELF-ESTEEM

It was Halloween, and my 11-year-old daughter – in costume – was admiring herself in the mirror. I've seen her do that before, when she is wearing something she particularly likes. It's something I actually *love* to watch her do, because she is always pleased with what she sees in the mirror.

She is always pleased with what she sees in the mirror.

WHOA!

Can you say that about yourself?

I've watched her do that many times before. New shoes, a dress she picked out, fancy earrings, a hairpiece or hairdo … her bikini … or even just a face-painted design. It's particularly fun for me when she puts together an ensemble or certain 'look' – she is so proud of herself, so happy with what she came up with, and how she looks in it.

And I'm happy to see that. So very, *very* happy.

It was my admiring her self-admiration this morning when a few things really hit me. I'll say the first thing again: *She is always pleased with what she sees in the mirror.*

I'm not. I never have been, at least as far as I can remember; *however,* my father might tell you something different. One of the many things he told me regularly when I was younger that I was vain; his famous line was that "Susie is so vain. She can't walk by a mirror without admiring herself." He still says that now, in past tense.

He was both right and wrong. A mirror did stop me – but it was not for admiration; it was for a checkup, to make sure what I wanted hidden or camouflaged was hidden or camouflaged. I was almost never admiring myself, because I was almost never happy with what I saw in the mirror – even at my daughter's age.

I was told regularly that I was fat, and in a variety of creative ways: "You'd better lay off the ice cream, Cheeks." and "I don't understand how those legs of yours can hold you up!" and "Fat people are the loneliest people in the world." and (if I reached for seconds at the dinner table) "Do you really need that?" I remember one time my aunt had mentioned that I lost weight. She said to my father, "Don't you think so?" His answer? "Yes. But I'm not going to tell her that; she'll stop."

I have to point out that this is not complaining. This is a simple recounting of what happened. The one thing I had and have always known is that my father's intentions were and are always in the right place – he just went about it wrong (yes, I am saying that). I even told him that back then that I needed encouragement, not 'breaking,' but Dad was a drill instructor who'd had his own brand of parenting (like all people). He did the best he could with what he had. As angry and as hurt as I would get about the things he said – and as many times as I would try to get through to him without success, I would console myself a teeny bit with the thought: "He's an idiot."

Being happy with how you look is not vanity. Caring *only* about how you look is.

As children, we learn about the idea of being happy with ourselves in stages. How we look is first. Think about it, what were the first five years or so of our lives about? What did we hear all the time? "Oooh … she's/he's *adorable!*" "How cute is she/he?"

Our first frame of reference for judging ourselves is our appearance. Kids believe they are 'cute' and 'adorable' and 'beautiful' because that's what everyone told them, all the time. Then they get a little older and go to school and begin to hear other things; they begin to understand the barrage of advertisements on the radio and television and learn about what makes certain celebrities so popular. Then, they make comparisons between themselves and others.

The second stage is usually learned as a consolation: "She may be very pretty/thin/popular, but she's not a nice person, and being nice is important."

Well, that always made me feel better.

Being happy with yourself is not about how you look; it's about how you feel about yourself as a person – but none of us realize that until well after childhood, when we've had relationships (romantic, friendships, and work- or team-related) and we've had the chance to experience other types of contrast.

An initial negative self-image sets the stage for more negativity. No, I couldn't walk past a mirror without stopping for damage control – and all I saw when I looked was my flaws, something that got worse as I got older and knew there were more to see.

Positive self-image starts somewhere. Children are set up with all the 'oohing' and 'aahing' and 'awwws' they hear. When they start thinking to believe it, *let them*. Even when they choose an outfit that is mismatched, or want to wear a Batman cape to school every day – even if you yourself think they look fat in that bathing suit (you can be honest with yourself, right? Remember, you've been programmed, too).

When children start off admiring themselves in mirrors, they will be more likely to *continue* looking for what they like in them, rather than looking for things to tear apart.

Tell them they are smart. Praise them when they show foresight. Encourage them to think positively about everyone around them. Teach them that opinions of others don't need to affect them (without being too harsh on others). Let them know that what they like is perfect for them, and should never be changed just to please someone else. Pay attention when they show an interest or passion in something and encourage it.

But remember, their first 50,000 compliments and words of encouragement all had to do with how they looked. Let them be happy with how they look. Let them make decisions on what *they think* looks good for them. They will learn to make the 'what's right for them' choices a little earlier, even with outside differences of opinion – that starts off smaller at younger ages, and they can learn it in small bites. Then, they will grow into making more and bigger 'what's right for them' choices.

This *will* change the programming. It's up to us to support it – despite our own ingrained 'stuff.'

Think it doesn't matter? I grew up believing I was fat and stupid. I hated myself, all the way up until I began to see that I did not have to accept others' opinions of me as my own – and then, I had to fight myself to stop believing it (and I'm fighting still). That's taken a lot of time. Having to spend time erasing takes time away from moving forward.

Four months ago, I was with my father, and he made a reference to me being skinny. When I say it stopped me in my tracks, I am totally understating how it affected me. I said to him later that I never (*never*) thought I would hear him say that about me. He said in surprise, "That was thirty years ago!"

He and I will probably not always see eye to eye. We grew up with different experiences and different types of programming. He may not even believe in programming the way that I do. Because I am me, if he ever sees my daughter admiring herself in a mirror and dares to comment on it (and I know he will), I will probably feel compelled to line up more mirrors so she has more to look at (and *he* knows *I* will)!

There is much more to being happy with yourself than just how you look – but it has to start somewhere. I struggle to make sure my daughters don't have the same poor body image that I had/have. My older daughter doesn't have a great body image, but it is better than mine was. Maybe my younger's will be even better.

Let children love themselves – every single part of them. Relearn the first love you had for yourself before you were taught there was less to love.

I'm seeing a resemblance of my father's vanity comments in the many arguments against selfies. Is it a sign of insecurity to post a picture of yourself when you think you look good? Do people post selfies on social media only to get attention? Doesn't a supposed insecurity stem from the perception of what others think and why? Again, remember that despite how far we've come along in this world, every child learns a big measure of their worth first in their appearance – and it *is* appearance. Let them post their selfies when they feel they look good; eventually they will begin posting them more no matter how they look as they begin to feel more comfortable with so-called acceptance.

If you are concerned about their esteem, pay attention to their use of photo filters and see if they are posting themselves as they are or as they think they should look – either way, *pay attention to them.*

Let them learn to state to the world, "I think I look good and that's all that matters!" We are all allowed to take pride in being happy with how we look; we are allowed to *love* every aspect of ourselves. How we look may only be just one aspect, and not as important as other traits we have — but as the first we learned about, it is quite significant.

Look in the mirror. Smile. Be happy with what you see. All of it. It's all yours.

11 MY HONOR IS AT STAKE

I'll never forget the day someone told my parents that I'd had sex.

I was 48.

A rather explicit and graphic email describing me having sex with someone I had dated when I was 19 was sent to my parents

- and my brother and sister

- and my 22-year-old daughter.

When I read the email, I thought I remembered the sex to be better than described – and if my then-boyfriend turned out to be gay (as also mentioned in the email), that that had nothing to do with me.

But what do I know? I was 19 and I wasn't all that experienced. I'm quite sure sex I have now is better, so he could be right about that. And so what if the guy turned out to be gay; I still had sex, right?

The man who sent the email was not my former boyfriend, but someone who used to live in the same apartment building with him.

This man later married one of my family members. He and his wife extricated themselves from our family years ago after they both became financially successful. They determined that their 'white trash' families (on both sides) had no continuing value to them and that they suffered terrible childhoods at our hands. Therefore we should be banished from their lives.

All was quiet for a number of years until – and I'm guessing here, because no one actually spoke to us – they began having trouble with each other. My family received a 'farewell' email from this man who referred to his wife by her maiden name and then another that blamed all of us for their troubles, saying that we needed to be punished.

He was insulting, of course, and his attack was vicious, personal, and very detailed (notice the word 'accurate' is missing). I responded by sending his email back with grammatical and contextual corrections. Hence, the sex email.

When I read it, I'm not even sure what I felt. On one hand, I felt bad for my family – especially my daughter – for having to read that kind of shit; I know it would horrify a lot of other people. But I thought about it; my family (as fucked-up as I've said we are) is actually pretty cool. We've been through a lot together. *Together* being the operative word. We have our own bond, and still manage to love each other even though we know the individual foibles of each member. That really does mean something. My family knows that I am fully capable of making myself look like a fool better than anyone else can, so this email couldn't make them think any worse of me. While it may not have been enjoyable for any of us to read such a missive, the facts that the events described happened 30 years ago lessened any shock value – again, they know me; if I'm an idiot now, I was a bigger idiot when I was younger. Plus, I have two kids; I'm sure they've all figured out that I've had sex.

In his vicious attack he threatened the entire family, declaring war in writing with the caveat "My mind, my time, my wealth aimed at YOU. Get ready!"

Because I'm still an idiot, my first thought was to be flattered that little old me could ever deserve such attention.

Then, I thought, *Wow. That's a real threat.* I don't think I ever expected to get one in my life. At least, not since high school.

I guess I'm a late bloomer.

I started to ponder this. Should I be worried about this? Could this person hurt me and my family?

I suppose. Maybe. Yes. No. All of the above. That person has enough free time and considerable resources, so I guess if the desire is there it is possible to cause some trouble, at the very least.

What could happen to me?

- My reputation could be ruined? *Been there; done that.*

- Could I be financially ruined? *It be hard to break down something that was never there.*

- Would another wedge be driven into my family? *I'm Sicilian; we do wedges better than lettuce and Dr. Scholl's combined.*

- Is it possible that this person could ruin my attempts at fulfilling my dreams of becoming a full-time writer? *As if anyone one can shut me up. Ask anyone who knows me. And if you are reading this …*

I guess all that's left is my honor. So, I guess that is what is at stake.

That's a funny line, isn't it? "My honor is at stake." What, am I a sixteenth century virgin?

I think we've already covered that I'm not a virgin.

But what is honor? Is it high respect? Esteem?

I guess the idea of worrying about my honor boils down to whether or not I feel something could happen that might make someone lose respect for me. What THAT boils down to is whether or not someone else's opinion of me matters. I don't say that in belligerence, and I certainly don't deny that my feelings could never get hurt; what I am saying is that I have the right to only be concerned with what I think of myself. Everyone has that right.

What do I think of me?

For answers, I went to the family closet and danced with a few of my skeletons. I found quite a few that I would probably be happier if they stayed where they were, and not publicized in gory, Technicolor detail.

Wow. There are more than I thought.

(No. I didn't murder anyone, nor do I have any plans to.)

But, boy! Did I do some stupid shit! Of course, I don't believe I could have gone a full 51 and a half years without amassing a pile, right?

This particular theme of worrying what others think about and their judgment of me has been an ongoing theme of mine over the years. I've realized how much less I worry about what others think as I've aged, and that it seems to have taken getting older to let go of that concern.

If what others think about me doesn't matter, all that's left is what I think of me. So, what do I think about me? Oh, I'm an idiot. I've been childish, selfish, mean, pathetic, stupid, ridiculous, hurtful, snide, lazy, messy … I could probably go through the alphabet at least three times (and all of the seven dwarfs).

Then again, I'm also not as insecure as I used to be. I'm happier than I used to be. I'm learning more than ever, and that's allowed me to appreciate more. I even get proud of myself once in a while. (Yay, me.)

Would a smear campaign take any of that away? No.

I would probably be embarrassed, though.

Why?

Why, indeed? Because I've done things people wouldn't have expected me to do? Because I've surprised someone else – or, better yet, because I've *disappointed* someone?

Humiliation needs to be accepted. If I feel ashamed for something I've done, that is on me. Am I proud of everything I've done? Of course not. Sometimes, I even try *not* to repeat the same mistakes over and over. If I let someone make me feel humiliated, that is on me, too. For me to accept humiliation, I would have to believe that another person has more value than I do, and if I've learned one thing, it is that I am just as wonderful as everyone else.

I may have to remind myself of that once in a while. I do still have some residual insecurities carrying over from my childhood that rear their ugly heads every so often. But I'm getting better at recognizing them as old perceptions that don't serve me anymore. Whether or not I have my shit together is irrelevant; none of us do completely, and if we are all still wonderful then I'm in pretty good company.

I was never good at measuring up to anyone else's yardstick, and I realized it's a waste of time to try. If each day I can do one thing better, nicer, or smarter than I did the day before, then I can be happy with myself, no matter what anyone thinks. We all can.

What anyone thinks of me, or however they try to influence what others think of me really doesn't matter. I'm still going to get up every day and carry on with my life. I'm not trying to be brave. If others can be influenced in any way to turn against me then they were never for me. Everything I've done, I've done. Good, bad, or otherwise. I'm being *real*. I try to be better each day. I try to enjoy the life I have. I voice my opinions, relevant or not. I talk about sunshine, love, connections – about what I would like to achieve, what I aspire to.

And I *still* do stupid shit.

Duh.

I stopped responding to this person, despite a continuous attack carried through the internet, postal service and Ma Bell. I will take whatever action I need to defend myself, if needed, but nothing in retaliation. What he says to other people about me doesn't matter to me; if it matters to them, that's their issue. It's not like I have the monopoly on issues.

Do I argue? Some would say incessantly. My one snarky response was wrong (even if I found it clever), but I will not engage in his war. I have other things in life more valuable to worry about than a perceived sense of my honor as considered by others. I'm not always right; but I'm learning to be right with me.

Who knows? I might even learn from this.

Then, without even going into battle,

I win.

12 THE GOD I SERVE

Common rules of etiquette discourage discussions of politics or religion in polite company. While I've never been considered 'polite company' and my adherence to any form of etiquette is usually questionable, I have learned that if I want to get along with people in general, it is helpful to keep that guideline in mind. Unfortunately, there are times when it is unavoidable; people are who they are because of their beliefs. I can avoid the subject of politics easily enough because my belief (or current disbelief) in my country's choice of president has nothing to do with who I am, but my 'religious' (for lack of a better word) beliefs do. When what I do, say or am comes into question, the answer always tunnels down to my beliefs and my religion – or presumed lack of.

Religion, faith, and beliefs are wonderful to have – and we all do, whether or not any of us realize we are acting on them; they are all basically the same idea, too, but the word 'religion' seems to take precedence over the others because having a name for your religion, being able to label it, makes it easier for others to determine the right way to judge you.

I belong to no organized religion. To me, the idea of organization in religion is limiting. When you organize your room you limit the mess; when you organize religion, you limit *faith*.

This brings into question the God I Serve. For the record, the idea of 'serving' anything rankles. There are better actions to take to enjoy a fulfilling and giving life, and better words to describe the way a good life is lived.

What god do I serve? What god do I believe in? According to most, there is only one GOD. Despite my apparent contradictions, I agree, although I hesitate to use the term GOD because the widely-held definition is a little too organized for me. The one God that I believe exists is less limited in scope, ability, knowledge, and *love* than pretty much every definition I have been taught to believe – God more than a compilation of all gods, and so much more expansive than the common words and labels used to describe God (which, in and of themselves are more expansive than even the belief-actions used to support them).

Like everyone else, my first exposure to God came through the family I was born into. We went to church every Sunday, and repeated the same words each week. I never felt any connection to it; it was just something I had to do. I'm aware of some issues at home about it, when my father talked about the church wanting too much money from him. That was probably my first real thought about organized religion.

I believe that had to do with our leaving that particular religious branch. After my parents divorced, my mother went church-shopping. We tried on a number of different denominations and finally found one that fit, that made us part of their family – so much so, that we spent 4 days a week there between church services, age-specific classes, and youth groups. I resented the full immersion, but I liked that I felt I was actually learning about God and a reason to go to church. I really liked the new friends I made. I was in middle school and my three closest church friends were also in my classes. For three years, that church was the center of our lives.

It was also in control of our lives. We weren't allowed to do anything the church didn't allow. Two of the main rules that directly affected me the most were the rules regarding dancing and going to movies: we weren't allowed to do either. Now, school dances were a big part of middle school – even during the school day, occasionally. My mother would send a note to the school saying that I couldn't participate, and I would sit in the music teacher's class or the office until the end of the day (those dances were held during the last two periods) – until I stopped telling my mother, or stopped passing in the notes. I'd get in trouble and mom would send me to speak to the pastor. Our conversations were always the same: I would say, "What's wrong with dancing?" He would say, "What's good about it?" I would say, "I love it. It's fun." Then, we'd pretty much stare at each other for the remainder of the time I was there. I'm guessing he had trouble telling a 12 year old girl that dancing leads to fornication (my mother passed on that little tidbit to me). I was still a virgin at the time who had spent most of my life dancing – music and dancing was the one thread that never broke in my family – and, despite the fact that I was well into my masturbatory years I never associated dancing with sex; I didn't get the urge to 'play' after dancing, nor did I ever feel the need to play some music and dance to get me in the mood.

My mother eventually gave up on the dance battle, but held her ground about going to see movies. We were told that no matter what movie you went to see, the proceeds from the 'good' movies went in to making the 'bad' movies. This was all happening during the late 1970s and early 1980s when society was putting a particular focus on divorce, children from 'broken' homes, latchkey kids, and 'weekend fathers'.

What did weekend fathers do to entertain their children? They took them to movies. That was almost the staple back then. At first, my sisters and I told him we couldn't go. We did eventually go to the movies with him – and not because of pressure from him. We went to see *Lady and the Tramp*. It was actually funny how my mother found out.

My little brother was about 4 years old. He was sitting on my mother's lap, and my two sisters and I were sitting around her on the couch. He started singing the Siamese Cat Song from the movie. I'll never forget the first look on her face, the surprise and pleasure at his singing. Mom started singing along with him and when they finished she exclaimed, "I didn't know you knew that song! Where did you - ?" and then came that second look that I won't forget, that look of dawning surprise and then anger.

If my parents hadn't already been divorced by then, that probably would have finished them off. I won't forget the fight about it, either.

Nearing the end of our three years with that church, there were many arguments about it, between my parents and between us kids and our mother. I *was* learning about God, but I was learning about a rigid God that didn't like to be questioned, and I had many questions.

In the end, God – or God-through-the-church – decided we weren't worthy to be part of that family. My mother, who was welcomed into the fold as a divorced woman, was kicked out when she committed the sin of remarriage. By rights of relation, her children were also disinvited – and *shunned*. The 'family' that I'd known for three years had disowned us – even my friends had to stop talking to me. I was 13. That left quite an impression. I was told later that I would be welcome back in the church – but only as a guest, and only if I admitted my mother's sin of remarriage.

No, thank you.

After church-shopping once again, Mom found another religious branch to settle into. By then I was questioning everything – or, rather, I consider it the beginning of thinking for myself. I went to church, listened to what was said, and eventually went with what I felt my heart was saying believing *that* came from God. I stopped going to church, because with all the shopping we'd done I'd come to the conclusion that I believed they all worshipped the same God, but each had different ways of going about it. The rules each church called 'God's Rules' didn't make sense to me, because what was said about

God didn't make sense. I saw it every time my mother changed churches; she prayed differently, spoke differently, and would become immediately adherent to new sets of rules.

There is a distinct dichotomy to what is said about God and how He is represented by His People, in His Name. To kill, shun, harm, hate, disregard, deny, denigrate, judge, and punish other people In His Name? Love, All, Everything, Omnipotent, Omnipresent, Eternal, Creator … these are all 'limitless' words that describe a God whose power apparently isn't, if everything else taught is to be believed.

God created all. All. All is everything. Everything means that He created this *and* that. Here and there. Then and now. This and everything else.

Heaven *and hell.* Good *and bad.*

All of it. This and its opposite are the same thing, because you can't have one without the other. You can't know light if you don't know darkness. It is the polarity that allows the existence of anything. Good would not exist if there were no evil, because good is only good in its relation to evil.

Did we create the evil? The polarity? The darkness?

The Devil?

Isn't the boss responsible for the actions of his employees? In business, we don't allow the boss to claim ignorance of what the people who work under him are doing – but God can? So, God created everything – except those things?

How can there be a Devil? We are supposed to believe that this all-powerful deity is concerned of losing a battle with something of his own creation? That this entity is actually powerful enough to worry God? Remember all those expansive words used in describing God? Even if there were a Devil, wouldn't he still be a lesser being? Nobody calls the Devil all-powerful, yet somehow we should believe that he can overthrow God, or that an all-powerful and all-knowing God-that-has-it-all is worried that he can be overthrown. The Alpha and the Omega, the beginning and the end, is worried about the middle?

As far as we've been told, the battle between God and the Devil is fixed – it has already been won by God. This would mean the Devil has been paid or coerced into throwing the fight – he must, if we are to believe that he is or has ever been strong enough to win. And yet God still walks around like a sore loser, smacking down his children that may mis-play/may have mis-played possibly costing him the game.

Hell, if we're going to assign negative human traits to God, let's not cherry-pick which bad traits he has – we all know that a bad person is completely bad, right? It's always one or the other, isn't it?

We are also told that we need 'saving'. From what? If God created all things, and God doesn't make mistakes, *and he already won the battle,* what is there for him to have to save us from? Who is he saving us from, if everything comes from him?

Do we need to be saved from temptation? What is temptation? Temptation is the wanting to make a choice of the bad over what is good, and good and bad are relative to your beliefs. What is it that makes the 'bad' choice more desirable? Our thoughts? Where do our thoughts come from (or where are they supposed to come from)? Our church? Why were we given our own if we are not supposed to use them? Think about those 'studies' on children who were sat at a table and a plate of Oreos (or some other snack they liked) was put in front of them that they were told not to eat. What did they do when the adult left the room? Would you give your child an electric train set for Christmas and not let her play with it? Why not?

So, why would God do that to us? To give us our individual feelings, thoughts and abilities and not want us to play with them?

That is what Hell is to me; the denial of self. The flaming Hell after death could only exist if God's love was conditional. Hell is our own creation, either by repeating patterns that we know hurt us or by denying who we are. The country-music-loving teenager who pretends to like metal to impress her friends denies what she truly enjoys just to be part of a group or accepted. Is she happy listening to music she doesn't like? Is it right for her to sacrifice her own choice for the benefit of others? At some point, won't she resent what she has 'given up' in the name of acceptance?

To me, the idea of a God is everything that I've heard said about all of them – at least in the sales pitch. The Eternal, the Life Force, the Universal Creator, Love. *All.* The words used to describe the indescribable. How can we reconcile the expansive meaning of the word God with the limited qualities of neediness, jealousy, judgment, intolerance, separation, bias, and control? What I find hard to believe is all of the negative human traits that have been ascribed to a being or force that is not human, as well as the "God works in mysterious ways" cop-out when questions can't or won't be answered. It's a little too "because I said so" for me.

I feel that the idea of God-the-parent came about as a means of explanation – the easiest way to explain a large idea is to bring it down in terms easily relatable. Unfortunately, we have the habit of taking the easiest explanation and building a whole story around it, even if the initial comparison was used solely as an example, and we pigeon-hole it right there, forgetting we were talking about something much larger.

My own father used the fear-based parenting method, which is basically the method of the God who threatens eternal damnation for disobedience. Before I knew anything about God, I *knew* my father's method was … not right. Learning of a God who parented the same way was both confusing and disillusioning. I had time to rethink my opinion again when I became a parent. The only thing that changed was my understanding of *why* my father chose that method. I even called him to let him know that while I still disagreed with it, I did understand it. It's definitely easier to keep kids in line when they fear you.

By 'keeping kids in line' and expecting them to follow a set path we give them no opportunity to grow. If learning is a result of doing, what chance would they have to learn more than we know if that is the limit of what we allow them to do? What of mistakes? Aren't mistakes considered the ultimate teachers? Yet the only way to make a mistake is to step out of line. How then can we preach of a God who allows no room for growth? What would be our purpose here?

We can't be here to learn if we are not allowed to color outside of the lines and think for ourselves. Life cannot be a school if all we are taught is imitation and limitation. Here, again, we take an oversimplification and get stuck in it. Look how our educational system has changed, and how our beliefs about our educational system has changed – including what is being taught. We see that children from families with money have more advantages than those that don't, and that schools in certain geographical areas are better than schools in others. We are aware that children need a basic education and that childhood education is not consistently basic across the country. If life is indeed a school and we only have one shot at taking the standardized test, a fair God would have created a level playing field, with every child having the same opportunity, background, and physical and mental ability. Even those who believe that 'everyone will be told the message of God and allowed the chance to repent before they die' have to admit that those who were born being 'told the Truth' have an unfair advantage over those that weren't. Maintaining a belief is easier than changing one.

It is said that God doesn't make mistakes, but it's also said that we are born in sin. Who screwed that up? Because we have been born in sin we must spend our lives making up for the mistakes of whom? Isn't the sinner a mistake? Is that fair, to punish all for some? How, then, can anyone truly believe they are one of God's Special Creations with that kind of burden hanging overhead? Are we special, or not? Are we loved, or not?

Ask any new mother about her baby, her *perfect* baby. The child is told of his perfection immediately – not one relative or well-meaning friend visits the child for the first time and points a finger at that child yelling, "Sinner!" How would the mother react? And that same mother will turn around later and tell her child, her *perfect* child, that he is *not* perfect?

It's hard to accept the idea that an all-powerful, all-knowing, God-who-has-it-all would need to create the unworthy, and task them with a lifetime of trying to earn worthiness with the threat of eternal damnation if they don't succeed. For what purpose? If he wanted us to be a certain way, wouldn't he just have made us that way?

What kind of God would demand perfection out of the imperfect? What kind of God would enjoy watching his creations struggle to be perfect, to vie for his attention? Does he sit back during the most fervent prayers looking to see who 'wants it the most'? Would God only mete out miracles or cure someone when he 'felt like it'? Which cancer patient is more worthy than the other? What makes him more worthy?

The God(s) that I have been told about give us choices we are not allowed to make, punish us for sins we didn't commit, love us conditionally, and threaten us unless we toe a certain line (out of many). A puppet-master whose sole reason for creation is need for adulation and control. And the puppets should love him?

If God is love, and the oft-cited 1st Corinthians 13 is true, then there is no way we were created for the sole purpose of worshipping and proving our devotion to this God because "Love is not self-seeking … it keeps no record of wrongs." This also denies the thought that God seeks to punish us for not worshipping Him.

We talk about jealousy and what a negative trait it is – especially in relationships. And we also hear it celebrated that our God is a jealous God, and we are in relationship with Him.

I'll be honest, it makes no sense to me that I've been told I should worship a God who has all the qualities of a man I won't date.

I believe that we, and everything around us, are connected. We are both the parts of the whole, and the whole itself. The idea of us being created in God's image means we are created as Him. Like a hologram, you have the whole image, but if you cut out even a small piece of that hologram you still have the whole view of the entire holographic image.

The Holy Trinity (God the Father, God the Son, God the Holy Spirit), the triune - the three that are one - they are the id, ego, superego and the conscious, subconscious, superconscious. The mind, body, and spirit of each individual. Separate, but whole and part of a whole.

Am I saying that we are Gods? In essence – and at the risk of being crucified – yes. We are the creators of the time and space we hold ourselves limited to, we are the creators of our realities. What each of us believes is what is, because we act our lives out based on those beliefs – whether or not they are true to others. We are the expression of God in the multitude of forms a God can take; this is how God knows he/she is God.

"For now we see reflection as in a mirror" is another part of that chapter on love in 1st Corinthians. When you know yourself, you will know God; know yourself and you will be known. Like the definition of the word *'Namaste'* the spirit in me recognizes the spirit in you. The 'still small voice' of God is your own inner voice, your gut instinct, your intuition, and your own inner truth. We have been told "Ye are Gods" – although the definition of the word God changes a few times in the passage it is taken out of. *All this that I can do, you can do also.*

We play the game of Follow the Leader as children, where we mimic everything the leader does, and later learn contradictory statements like 'those who can't do, teach'. Books on leadership skills profess that the best way to lead your employees is to know what their job is; leading other people is about showing them what they can do. Following a leader is not about blindly doing what the leader says to do; it's about following the leader's methods and actions. Employees respect their employers more when they know they do not consider themselves above the work being done in the trenches. The best bosses help shape employees to become bosses themselves, otherwise there would be no parameters for promotion. We are coming to see that employee morale matters in performance; encouraging employees to want to do and enjoy their jobs will make them better employees. Those that come up with solutions not previously considered are praised. We know that job ability is not regulated by words written on specialty paper or the right words stated in an interview.

Society has decided that discrimination is wrong. If you are not an equal-opportunity employer you can be sued. Letting *all* of the kids on the team play the game is fair. We should never judge a book by its cover. Be happy. Be who you are.

Be who you are, because God-who-doesn't-make-mistakes made you that way, and you are perfect. It takes many different wires to conduct energy in an electrical box, it takes different spices to make a sauce, each instrument in an orchestra needs to produce a different sound to create a symphony, and it takes different people to create new opportunities.

All of the qualities we are teaching to succeed in business and in life are the opposite of the childhood follow-the-leader qualities we are told best 'serve God' – at least the God of many organized religions who is judgmental, exclusionary, intolerant, needy, jealous, narcissistic, and unfair.

Do unto others as you would have done unto you. What you do for the least of you has been done for me. Remember the Sabbath and keep it holy. I am the still small voice. Ye are Gods. All that I can do, you can do also. Now I know in part, then I shall know fully, even as I am fully known.

We are Gods. We are the creators. Individually we create our own heaven and hell as parts of our collective Universe. The Sabbath is the day or time we take to relax, to reflect, to reconnect with the highest part of ourselves, the force that connects all of us as one.

Our connections are visible in instances of mob mentality, when people are considered to be of the same mind, in those who finish each other's sentences, at a music concert where people of different walks of life are all swaying to the same beat. God is in us and the energy between us. The *all*.

When I speak of God using that name, this is what I'm referring to. My idea of church and fellowship is spending time with people who are loving and true to themselves, those of us who can move mountains by our mutual support of each other with allowances to the individual spirit of each that enhances the group: *where two or three are gathered together in my name* – that name of the life force in and among us, our separate part of the whole and our wholeness.

Namaste.

13 WHOSE SEXUALITY IS IT, ANYWAY?

My older daughter grew at a faster pace than most girls her age. Because of this, she was sent home from school more than once because of an outfit of hers that was deemed 'inappropriate' – even though all of the Dress Code guidelines in the school handbook were followed to the letter. In fact, we took the time every single school day to *measure* skirt and shorts lengths and shoulder strap widths. What a waste of time that was if I still had to take time out of my day to go to her school to argue with the Vice Principal about her clothing. Why? The answer I got from the vice principal was that her outfit "looked different on her" than it did on other girls in her class.

- how fucking stupid was he to actually come out and say that? I guess that depends on your perspective, doesn't it? Just *how* was her teacher looking at her?

Is that her fault? Is it her fault if she looks 'different' in her outfit than other girls do?

School dress codes are the most insidious form of female objectification because they are enforced the moment girls begin their first real social interactions. What they are taught by schools is that they are responsible for thoughts and actions of others, and that that responsibility is more important than their own education.

How funny is it that we are taught that we are powerful enough to distract other people from their studies or cause them to act out in lustful delirium, and at the same time told that have no real power when it comes to matters of authority? Which is it? One would think if we were truly that powerful, all men would be cowering at our feet from the moment we all turned 10.

One of the most common arguments in favor of the dress code is that there should be a standard of what's deemed appropriate. What standard would that be? Hide the sex organs?

If that were the case, then hands and mouths should be hidden, too. I don't know about you, but I use both of them during acts of a sexual nature. But they are not considered sexual. Why? Is it because they have other, primary, functions? Technically speaking, the body parts we have deemed sex organs (at least on the outside of the bodies) are not primarily for sex. Breasts are necessary for milk production and delivery. Both the penis and the vagina have other, more important uses that make any sexual traits secondary; you won't die from not having sex, but you will die without proper waste disposal.

Every little girl has that moment when she asks for her first bikini. When is told she can't have one, the reason is almost always that she is *too young*.

Too young for what? To be recognized as a girl? Why? Is that something she had control over? Is that something she should be ashamed of? That's effectively what we are telling them.

Do you know why most little girls want two-piece bathing suits? Because it's easier to go to the bathroom in them! You ladies know exactly what I'm talking about.

And yet the women's body is subjected to rules that imply ownership by anyone else other than herself.

Hide your boobies, honey; you're not old enough for them. They have a power that you are too young to know how to control.

Women are told that there are times and places for allowable breast visibility.

Show me your tits, honey!

-- Whoa – are you breastfeeding? That's disgusting! Put those things away!

We are taught that there are specific allowable times and circumstances that breast visibility is allowed:

1. First, she must be over the age of 18. We wouldn't want to send a man to jail because he was lured under false pretenses.

2. When tending bar. Boobs are a huge draw to the bar crowd.

3. In movies, music videos, video games, etc. i.e., for someone else's entertainment.

Breast visibility is not allowed:

1. During primary functional use. Breastfeeding ruins the male fantasy, and we can't have that, can we?

2. When the woman is over the age of 30 (unless her breasts are younger than she is).

3. When they 'belong' to someone else.

Little girls cannot show signs of having breasts or feminine figures, because little boys are taught that they are their playthings - and what little boy doesn't want his Christmas presents early? Any sign of sexuality is only allowed for someone else's entertainment.

We are teaching little girls that their bodies are not their own. Little girls' bodies are the devil to little boys, unfairly tempting them just by being there, distracting them from their school work, making them think all kinds of impure thoughts and act out aggressively.

Apparently, the only way to keep a boy out of trouble around girls is to hide the girls.

Yes, honey; it's your fault. Without even trying, you made little Johnny daydream about/ start at you during class and he did not pay attention enough to pass his test. Because of that, you are to be banished to your home until you learn that his grades are more important than yours. I'm sorry that you have breasts at your age. What was God thinking by giving them to you before you graduated high school? With all those boys we have to worry about getting promoted? We may have to stop your dance classes, too, if you want to still be able to wear shorts in the summer. You are too young for your legs to look like that.

The same people that tell us that women have to hide their sexuality are the same ones who applaud Hollywood's sexiest – that is, of course, if they are the right *age*. The boyfriend or husband who doesn't want 'his woman' to dress a certain way is the same one ogling the girl in the tight skirt. The *gentlemen* of old who would lay down their jackets over a puddle for a woman had wives *and* mistresses. The two men who would duel over a woman's virtue were the two who were interested in getting a chance at taking it – duels were never fought over the honor of a woman the men didn't know, or just women in general.

The fact that we were never told to 'sow our wild oats' says a lot. Even in the 50's, when a man stepped out on his wife, it was her fault. Alcoholism and abuse were not allowed to be spoken about. If a girl was raped, someone always said 'she asked for it.' A woman should go to her husband a virgin. If you terrorize people, you will win many virgins. Was a man ever told to worry about keeping his woman happy at home to make sure she didn't stray?

Sexuality wasn't something women were supposed to reveal, and sex wasn't something we were supposed to *like* (unless you were a slut, of course); it was something you had to keep carefully guarded until the time was right to 'gift' it to someone who didn't need to reciprocate in the same manner. For a long time we weren't allowed any powers, voices, or freedoms – yet our sexuality would be used against us in justification of the thoughts and actions of others.

For the record, *anything* can be viewed as sexually attractive, by *anyone*, at *any* time. It is not about the object that is found desirable, it is about the person looking at the object. And that is solely the responsibility of the observer, and not what he or she is looking at. It is time to stop giving girls the mixed signals about sexuality and sex, and the blame (and shame) for being female.

Let me tell you a secret: I happen to think that men's forearms can be sexy. Since I may or may not be a sexual deviant, and because I may not be the only one who thinks like this, wouldn't it be wise now to make sure all boys start wearing long-sleeved shirts? (#coverthosearms)

What this has done to us is to make us afraid for our daughters, attempting to curb their own exploration of body-consciousness and self-esteem by instilling in them that girls always have to worry about what and how other people are going to think about them. Only a mother would understand the torment of trying *not to* come out and say to a very little girl, "You can't wear that because men might look at you the wrong way." But when that little girl gets older that is exactly what we tell them. How do we raise girls that are brave, with a strong sense of self and positive self-esteem, if we instill the fears on them that we were brought up with that other people's thoughts and actions are allowed to dictate their lives? How can we teach them that their bodies are nothing to be ashamed of?

Has it crossed anyone's mind that maybe if young girls were allowed to be and explore their sexuality as it came up naturally and not on someone's time schedule, that Halloween would have less sex appeal? Of course girls are going to dress 'like that'; it's the only night they don't have to be what everyone else expects them to be.

Everything about our bodies has been under someone else's jurisdiction. That is the main blockage to healthy self-esteem, body-consciousness, and self-love – and it is the first blockage. Remember that the baby's first praise has to do with looks. When a girl's body starts changing and she has to worry about how she looks to someone else — to *everyone else* — she will never be able to accept herself fully as she is, because she will always disappoint someone.

The worst of the fallout of the debated ownership of women's sexuality is the in-fighting that is happening between women. The social, familial, and religious imprinting of what is 'proper' for a woman is so generationally ingrained that many of us are unaware of how much we've bought what was sold to us. We then attack each other for breaking the unwritten laws of others that should have no bearing on how we live our lives. You aren't beautiful unless you are a certain size and look a certain way. Self-expression, self-confidence, and self-esteem are not as important as what others think about you.

We follow the dress codes that are laid down for us, turning a blind eye to the fact that they were really just rules for girls, so that boys won't get distracted. We use the school dress code as the base model of the dress code we ourselves created for purposes of getting into the business world — more manly and complete with stick up ass. Basically, we decided that to be able to compete with men in the business world we had to hide the fact that we were girls (again), because everything that made us girls was just too sexual (as perceived by others) — and feminine sexuality (just being a girl) is not to be taken seriously in matters of business.

How'd that work out for you, Ladies? You bossy bitches, you!

Sexuality is in the eye of the beholder. We should be giving ourselves the permissions and respect of honoring and appreciating what we were born with, however that may be, and give other women that same permission and respect as well. But we can't because of our shame and our learned feelings of responsibility that healthy body-consciousness to us is sexual to another, and that is what we teach our daughters and enforce on other women around us.

We are catty to each other, and overcritical. Usually the first criticism of another woman has to do with how she dresses. When we attack the outfit of another woman it can usually be because:

- We were sold a vision of how it was supposed to look and who was supposed to wear it, and how dare she attempt something that Macy's says she's not qualified for?

- We are jealous – not because she 'looks better', but because we don't have appreciation for our own body type. We envy her confidence more than her visual appearance.

- We worry that she in that outfit could steal our man. (Forget that you are blaming her for the fact that your relationship is not stable.)

I hope you all noticed that *all of these reasons* are based in outside opinions – even the jealousy of the other woman's self-appreciation, because she 'shouldn't be able to feel that way'.

Ladies, do you remember when you were younger and thought everything was possible for you? Even if your childhood was not rosy, didn't you *believe* deep down inside that you would still win out in the end?

Do you remember the joy in wearing an outfit you felt really good/beautiful/confident in?

Do you remember, too, if you were made to feel any shame in it? What did that do to you? If that happened to you, then you must be totally aware of the power you have over your own daughter's self-view.

Every single group that has been under a forced oppression of any kind will usually reach a point where they fight back, and the weapons they use are those qualities or aspects of theirs that had been specifically denigrated. And they will do so in a big way. How many jokes had there been many years ago about how easy Catholic school girls were outside of school? Or divorced women?

Hell, the only reason any of us would even think to use sex as a weapon is because we grew up being shown that it was an effective one.

Why do women call each other 'Bitches'? Part of any fight against being marginalized is to first take over the language and wording. A woman was called a bitch as an insult. Now, we have taken that word, mocked it, and made it our own. There is no power to it anymore. (Think about that; there are other words that have been appropriated for the same reason. It's quite effective.)

The best way to disarm the enemy is to use their own words and weapons against them.

Another method is to take unwanted thoughts, behaviors, and speech to the extreme. You may not want to be as overtly sexual as Madonna, Beyonce, and Miley Cyrus, but they are doing all of us women a great favor by helping to desensitize the stigma against our being as 'sexual' as we want to be. And, they've given us all a little more room to move freely around in with less fear of judgment. Women will start to come out more when they see other women doing the same, and their fear will be lessened by the consolation that the small steps they take on their own are not as drastic as those pioneers.

I'm not condoning the battle of the sexes, I'm just pointing out the obvious. Race and gender rights ... *human rights* ... are being *fought* for. Still. That really is a shame. It would be nice to live in a world where we are all accepted for who we are, and allowed to shine as bright as we were meant to, *however we feel we were meant* to, without being told we were wrong for it. These battles are signs of people's desire for that change to occur. Eventually, we will work our way back into love. I do believe that.

But still, and despite all the steps we have taken forward, there is still a large measure of thought that women are 'second'. Thank you, Adam. How nice of you to give a rib to help create the woman that ultimately *distracted* you.

And now, we have more dress codes. Apparently, your age matters in choosing clothing more than whether or not those jeans still fit. You can't wear short skirts after age 30. You shouldn't wear this if you are a mother. You shouldn't dress like that if you are someone's wife. You're too young to wear that. You're too old to wear that.

Still, our validation and ability to be taken seriously is reliant on our dress and physical appearance first. What happened to the idea of dressing to express ourselves?

I guess we are only allowed to say so much.

I admit, it is tough when we are the parents of little girls and we know 'what's out there'. Even women have used the "she's asking for it" argument based on how a girl dresses. Yes, there are people who operate out of negative thinking. However, we can acknowledge the existence of the negative without marginalizing ourselves and our actions in deference to them – the bottom line is that girls get raped no matter what they are wearing or doing. It is not because of their clothing or how they look; it is because of what is in the other person's mind. We need to stop thinking that 'removing temptation' is better than fixing wrong thinking. The *standard* behind the dress codes is flawed because it makes one group responsible for another. I don't care how many years we've invested perpetuating it; maintaining a status quo because it's there is as bad as staying in an abusive marriage because of a document you signed – nothing gets better.

Changing a generations-old set of standards is not as hard as we think, either. In actuality, it will only take one generation – the newest group; if they are taught differently, all the rest that follow will be different.

But if you need to follow a dress code:

What Not to Wear

- Too-tight clothing: Clothing that interferes with your breathing is not good, because breathing is necessary for a lot of things.

- Stiletto heels: There's a time and place for high heels, even when you're not standing on them; however, they should never be worn when swimming, jogging, or skiing, they'll weigh you down, they don't have a lot of traction, and you could slip and fall. They should also not be worn when riding a motorcycle; it's just not practical.

- 'Mom Jeans': I hate to break it to you, ladies, you've been wearing Mom Jeans since you gave birth. If the jeans are hers, and she is a Mom, her jeans are Mom Jeans. Transitive Property. Do the math.

- Miniskirts: These should never be worn when walking a tightrope or climbing a ladder, because others will be able to see your underwear. It's probably not a good idea to wear them out in the snow either, because it's cold. Be careful on slides. Hot slides can burn - especially those old metal ones.

- Short-shorts: Like miniskirts, these should not be worn out in the snow, either; they are made for warmer weather.

- Long, dangly earrings: These can be dangerous if worn during sports or on rollercoasters – one could chip a tooth or poke an eye out.

- Flip-flops: See Stiletto heels. But please, please, don't wear socks with them. That's just wrong.

- Bright nail polish: If you wash dishes without gloves, or your hands are in and out of water a lot, bright nail polish isn't a good idea; this type of activity will cause the nail polish to chip faster, and bright colors show off chips more obviously than the blander colors.

- Sleeveless tops and dresses: If you have a sunburn on your arms and shoulders, you should not wear anything sleeveless if you are going back outside. Keep them covered until the sun goes down.

- Belly button rings: These may only pose a problem if you work a job with high-level security or spend a lot of time at airports, as some of the metal in certain jewelry pieces may set off alarms in metal detectors. Do you want to spend the extra time removing your belly ring while taking off your shoes, taking your laptop out of your bag, and emptying your pockets?

Imposed dress codes are not Universal Law. Ignoring them will not cause you any harm like, say, ignoring the Law of Gravity might.

Your *responsibility* is to wear whatever makes you happy at any time, for any occasion. What others think is their own.

14 THE DIFFERENCE BETWEEN SEX AND LOVE (MASTERING THE DEBATE)

I love sex! I *love* sex! I love *sex!* This has to be said by more people, especially women. The more this becomes 'accepted' – even if not totally acceptable – the less the idea of sex or sexuality belongs to anyone other than the person making the declaration.

Not too long ago, when a woman got married she used to be told to 'give in' to her husband's 'urges' – whether she liked it or not. Her virtue was his gift; since his virtue wasn't required at the time, the relationship was unfair from the start. We've evolved a little since then. A little. That advice morphed into, "Sex is a beautiful act between a husband and wife." Then, women were allowed to like sex, but only under certain conditions.

(For a little while in between it was, "Sex is a beautiful act between two people that love each other" – but that had to be changed because it started to give women too many options.)

117

It is possible to have sex without love. Anyone can. The person who believes it's impossible came by that belief through subconscious programming – that barrage of information he was fed throughout his formative years from his parents, his church, his schools, his media, and his society; This in turn causes his will (conscious and subconscious thought) to ignore sexual urges when they arise, or transfers that need (for lack of a better word) to something else. That *sexual urge* or compulsion starts in the body *without* thought, and well before a person learns about romantic love and is made aware of any association with it. The desire/urge/compulsion for physical pleasure is not the same as love - the love that we are taught we are to have with the person we are allowed to have intercourse with; they can intermingle, but neither requires the addition of the other.

Little boys *and girls* explore their bodies when they are very young, learning what things feel like and what feels good. When they find that touching themselves a certain way feels good, they will continue to do it joyfully – until they learn it is called *masturbating,* and get all the damning information about how shameful their bodies really are, and that that particular sinful act will surely land them in hell.

Actually, it will be hell more without it.

At the time of their discovery (before the beat-down) they have no knowledge that what they are doing is considered sexual, nor do they consider that anyone else is required to be a part of it. It doesn't happen when they are dancing, listening to Barney singing "I Love You", when they are drunk on cough syrup, or mildly sluggish on

Benadryl. It happens all by itself, exclusive of everything else, and quite naturally – and without the *love* they later learn must be associated with it.

It's when they are caught masturbating that they learn The Truth: their bodies are not for them to play with; they are for others to play with, under specific conditions.

And here's where I have to interject an already-mentioned thought that no parent would ever consider giving his child a gift that he wasn't allowed to touch. The body *is* a gift, but only to the soul living in it. It's your ball and you play with it your way. There is a way to play tennis by yourself.

This also harks back to the idea of more than one way to skin a cat. There is no one way to do *anything*.

If sex was not supposed to work outside of love, it wouldn't. Technically, it doesn't, if you can accept that pleasuring yourself is a form of self-love at its most natural. The idea of treating your body like a temple means that you take care of it and show it respect. Understanding your body and what it needs is the most respectful thing you can do for it.

I may be shot for saying this, but more than one person goes to a temple.

By taking care of your own needs – and knowing *you are allowed to* – you keep yourself in that position of conscious choice. You will not feel the lack of touch or the lack of physical pleasure that can drive

119

some people into Romantic Relationships that don't last. Sexual compatibility can keep people together – but only for a while. That Romantic Relationship that is borne out of a need for sexual pleasure (conscious or not) will not last – again, because once a need is met (or a goal is achieved), it is time to move onto the next one.

Another mindfuck of the tenet that sex can only be had as a part of love is that it can cause people to feel unlovable if no one finds them sexually desirable, and then they find more shame in their own bodies. That's where people start trying to look a certain way, whether it be an imitation of society's Sex Gods and Goddesses or just trying to look younger (following that myth that youth is more desirable). They will punish and starve their bodies trying to change for someone else, trying to change themselves into someone they feel they should be rather than who they are. If that doesn't work they become desperate and instead of attracting people, they end up pushing them away. This is where loneliness is born, out of the belief that someone else is *needed*.

Even if the methods of changing-yourself-for-another does work, the end result will still not be satisfying, because having to maintain what you think you should look like or be just to get someone or to keep someone around is exhausting and you won't be able to keep it up for long. You'll begin to feel an inner resentment because you will never feel like the *real* you is enough – and inner resentment becomes ever-present and interferes with your enjoyment of everything. Even sex.

Home is the place where you can let your hair down and be totally yourself, to relax and revive; making a home with someone you always have to be 'on' for will not feel homey for long. There are married couples out there who are not having good sex because they feel mentioning their likes and dislikes will turn their partner off. Denying your own sexual satisfaction will keep lessening your enjoyment of the act itself, eventually causing a loss of interest in it all together.

Or, it could make you just want to take matters *in your own hands*.

Either way, you lose the enjoyment of it with your allowed partner.

One of the sexiest qualities in a person is their own self-confidence. That is why needy and clingy people can be a turn-off. You don't want someone else to ever *need* you (again, once a goal is met …); you want a person who *wants* you, who selects you and has sex with you out of preference and choice – and who falls in love with you because of who you are. Romantic Relationships are about love and enjoyment, *not responsibility*. How exciting is it to feel the love of someone who chooses you for who you are and not because of what you can give them! You don't want to be with anyone, not even in a friendly way, who is after you for your money, right? *It's the same thing.*

Sex is *not* proof of love, nor is it a way to get that love of a Romantic Relationship. The best way to enter a Romantic Relationship is to do so when you are not in need of anything – and that includes body-pleasure.

There is the argument that sex is better with the one you love.

Duh!

So is going to the movies.

Everything is 'better' if you are doing it with someone whom you choose to be with, who you enjoy being with. As kids, did any of us like playing in the park with someone we *had to* play with because our parents were friends? What would we end up doing then? We'd end up playing *by ourselves*.

And we'd enjoy it. Because we chose.

We allow little boys their special time in the bathroom and clean their sheets without comment. Because it's normal. God forbid we allow and encourage little girls to take that kind of 'me time'. What? Little girls don't feel any urges to explore their own bodies and find out what works for them? Girls don't get those natural urges? I don't know when I began masturbating, but I have memories of it as early as age 7. I caught both of my daughters engaged in it around age 3. I also remember using items I found around the house to 'play with' –

- and I'm amazed that I never electrocuted myself.

Some children will be engaging in self-pleasure for *years* before they are told anything about sex and love and the *sin* of masturbation. The sense of guilt and shame that that can lay on a child is overwhelming. My mother didn't talk to me about sex at all directly; instead, she handed me a 4-book series called "The Life Cycle Library" – and not until I was 10, when I started showing signs of puberty. I'd been masturbating for at least three years before that. And it was three years after the books, at church, that I'd been disgracing myself before God, playing with what he gave me.

Despite popular opinion, the urge strikes girls at unusual times, too. I could be sitting at my computer (not dancing, not listening to soft music or Prince, no poster of Shaun Cassidy or Chris Pine or a current crush on my wall in front of me) and *feel* it. Also despite popular opinion, the idea that boys aren't the only ones who get horny is *known*. Why else would it be said that when a woman is acting uptight that she "needs to get laid" – that saying is *never* that she "needs to fall in love". Pregnant women are known to have an increase in their sex drive; even when their husbands are away at work.

It's not just 50-something divorcees who drink wine and own cats.

Age doesn't increase the libido, the knowledge of it does. Like Pavlov's dog we can have conditioned responses, but it starts with a natural urge.

Masturbation is very *instinctual* and begins before any association with love enters the picture. In order for children to grow into adults that are happy with their bodies, they should be allowed (and encouraged) to explore and enjoy their own bodies by themselves. If they learn to not be ashamed of any part of their bodies, they won't sell themselves short and settle into unhappy arrangements. They will learn that self-love is the most important, and that love is not something only received in a Romantic Relationship. They won't feel a need to look for it, either.

Love is all around us; we get it in many forms. It begins with self-appreciation, then parental and friendly love, even the love of our pets. We feel it for things we find beautiful and enjoyment we get out of life. When we see the love we have been receiving and the love we can feel for something or someone else, we don't feel that love is missing and needs to be sought after (thereby making sex a tool).

The idea that sex is only to be had with one person is also twisted thinking. We make connections of every kind throughout our lives and during different stages of our growth. We meet soulmates regularly, but we all change as our experiences change. We grow at different rates of speed. A soulmate is a person who fits you at the moment; if one of you changes or grows out of something – or stays stuck in something – the fit becomes less perfect. I'm not saying it's impossible to have one soulmate for a lifetime; I'm saying that by thinking it's necessary to look for *the one* causes a sense of desperation if we don't find it, makes us feel shame for making choices that didn't work out, and denies that soulmates are everywhere and found in many capacities. My best friend is my soulmate. *One of them.*

So, if sex and love aren't regulated as one thing, what then? Will people run amok, jumping on each other indiscriminately? Yes and no. The ones that will are the ones that are feeling the lack of it; the ones that won't feel that need are the ones that will go for what they truly want and not just what's in front of them.

It's like an all-you-can-eat buffet. The first time you go, you take everything and load up your plate. If you're starving, you start shoveling all of the food into your mouth; once you are not starving and beginning to feel full, you begin to be choosy about what you continue to eat, not selecting what you found you are allergic to (what is not compatible with your exact system), and what tastes the best to you (preference). And once you are full, you stop eating – even if there is more to eat in front of you.

The second time you go to the buffet, you only choose what you want and don't take more than you can eat.

What you choose at the buffet may change over time. I hated whipped cream as a child; I love it now.

Life is a buffet of experience. Sex is just one of those experiences. Mandating that sex can only be had or enjoyed under certain conditions puts pressure on people to act in ways they wouldn't choose to, and cause them to settle in lives that are less than what they imagined for themselves.

Sex and love are not the same. Sex does not make a relationship, but sexual incompatibility can ruin one. Love can be had without sex because love is an emotion, and sex can be had without love because it's a bodily function. Emotions heighten bodily functions, but don't cause them. Without restrictions on love or sex, we become selective and choose what is best for us. Having the freedom to choose what is best for us will ensure our happiness with our ability to love and be loved – as long as we know what's best for us. And we know what's truly best for us when we know how to love ourselves fully, including having no shame regarding our bodies.

Sex is not love and love is not sex. You can love yourself, and you can love others. I like going to the movies by myself, I love going with my friends. You can have sex by yourself because sex is nothing more than reaching an ultimate goal of body pleasure. The act of engaging in it with another person is an act of sharing pleasure by pleasuring each other. You scratch my back, I'll scratch yours — because we both want to, and not because I can't scratch the itch myself.

15 COURAGE

Bruce Jenner is now Caitlyn Jenner. And *she's beautiful.*

My, my. We've come a long way, baby, haven't we?

Our favorite leaders, artists, writers, singers … what makes them special is their nonconformity, their breaking free of the pack, their innovation. The innovators are the ones moving the world forward. What is an innovator? An innovator is the pioneer who *challenges and changes the norm.*

The people we revere in history were considered to be the rule-breakers.

Over the past thousands of years we have encountered many rule-breakers. These people – these innovators … these *teachers* … they make us *think* – by ourselves and for ourselves. People who've taught us about collective and personal freedom. Isn't that why America was born? Didn't our ancestors leave an oppressive atmosphere for the sake of freedom? What did we do with it? We united together to take away the freedoms of others.

127

What about those teachers? We revered them, then ridiculed them, and ultimately crucified them. Then later on we would look back and think, *hmmm … he wasn't so bad.*

Too late.

How is it that we can blatantly applaud the innovators, the rule-breakers, the people *who put their lives on the line to make our lives richer* and ridicule others who are making different changes? This selectiveness, this hypocrisy needs to stop. Because that is what it is. Are people only allowed to be different only because they do or make something a collective group deems to be useful or beautiful? What about the person who is able to create a beautiful life for herself? Is she wrong because she does not share your personal definition of what is beautiful and worthy?

Any person, situation, thought or idea that challenges the boundaries of exclusivity, privilege and intolerance benefits every single one of us.

Caitlyn should be praised for having the courage to stand up for herself, to be herself, knowing full well the backlash she would be up against. How many of us would have the balls (yes, I said it) to stand up to *global* ridicule?

She is a wonderful teacher for our children by showing them that no matter how old you are, how you've lived your life, that it is possible to change, to be real and *honest.* Aren't we teaching our children to be themselves? Be the best *YOU* you can be. Be *yourself.*

Or is that conditional?

Be you – *unless you are different.* If you are letting your children see your mockery of anyone who is not like you, what are you teaching them? How likely is it that they will find the courage to be who they are, if they are worried about the ridicule of others – even yours? Isn't the ultimate goal of a parent to see their child happy? Or does that depend on them being and doing what you or anyone else thinks they should be and do?

It had to be Bruce Jenner. There is not one other single person in the world who has gained the respect and attention of *the world* enough that this would reach *everyone.* He was a man's man, a superstar world athlete, handsome, father figure, and even reality show television star. He was also old enough that no one can accuse him of being a foolish child. *No one* hasn't heard of him – and that means *no one* can continue to keep their head in the sand and pretend to be ignorant of the word *transgender.* The line has been crossed, the tipping point reached, the pressure relief valve activated. We are now officially part of a new reality.

No one looks sideways when a woman votes or runs in the Boston Marathon. No one bats an eye walking into a classroom or getting onto a bus when they see varying degrees of skin color in the front seats. It wasn't always that way – and many people fought it and died because of it, but it is normal for us now.

It will still be a while before the LGBTQ community is no longer labeled as a separate, different sector of society. But we've hit another milestone, and it's a big one. From now on, the word transgender is a part of *world vocabulary.* No one can deny its existence.

129

This means we are one giant step closer to a new normal. We still have a long way to go. One person's sexual and gender orientation should never be the choice of or under the dictation of another person or group. There will still be fallout; people will still fight against this, and torment, torture and crucify those who are an active part of it.

And, maybe, some lives will be saved. Maybe another tormented soul will see the value in his or her own life, and stick around to make a positive difference in the world.

I'm going to die one day. So are the people who are actively against world peace, tolerance and love of thy neighbor. Even if they attempt to pass on their hate and segregation to their own children, it will be watered down and tempered by the fact that what was 'different' in their lifetime will be a known facet of the lives their children and grandchildren. It will not be different, which will make acceptance and tolerance easier.

I have three questions for you:

1. Bruce Jenner is now Caitlyn Jenner. How many of you lost your job or died because of it? Did it ruin your marriage? Are you gay now (if you weren't before)?

2. What if a transgender, gay, or any-sexual teenager decided not to commit suicide (despite all the bullying) and grew up to create the cure for cancer? Would you not allow your loved ones to take advantage of it because of where it came from?

3. If your Creator decided not to smite him for what he has done, what business is it of yours to try and do so? Isn't that usurping someone else's authority?

Another side of the idiotic controversy surrounding the new Ms. Jenner is the argument about whether or not she was courageous in what she did, because 'real' heroes are soldiers, veterans, cancer survivors, etc.

The Google dictionaries basically define the synonyms courage and bravery as "the ability to do something that frightens one" and "ready to face and endure danger or pain." A hero is defined as "a brave person."

Do you think Caitlyn Jenner didn't know the worldwide backlash she would get for what she did? You don't consider her moving forward in spite of that brave?

I wonder how many times you yourself have kept your mouth shut out of some type of fear of reprisal or repercussion (or even *personal discomfort*), and I wonder, too, if your own audience was as large as hers is?

What she did isn't as brave as a soldier fighting for our country? Or because she has money and a television show that makes her less brave? This whole "who is more courageous" argument is beginning to play out very much like locker room measurement conversation.

I'm going to be brave here – because I know full well that what I say next will piss some people off, and others will deliberately misunderstand the point I am going to make:

How is a soldier brave for *doing his job?* Something he or she signed up to do?

If that statement did in fact hit a nerve, you might want to consider whether or not you are just being a little too quick to judge without looking at a bigger picture. What I said is by no means any type of condemnation or denigration of their sacrifices, but it *is* a valid perspective. Just like every perspective is, and isn't.

Hey, I'm just playing devil's advocate here. We – myself included – need to stop tearing each other down. We need to be aware of the bigger picture. We need a little more perspective.

I have the utmost respect for the men and women in the military. I come from a military family and my brother served tours in Afghanistan and Iraq. And I salute you all for your bravery, because I can't honestly say I could do that.

Of course, now, if I stretched that last statement of mine further, I must be a coward, right? Because I won't engage in battle and fight for my country?

Let's go back to our definitions of courage and bravery:

"The ability to do something that frightens one; ready to face and endure danger or pain."

The ability to do something that frightens one.

Think about that.

Ready to face and endure danger <u>or pain</u>.

Think about that, too.

Do you fully understand what those two statements mean? It means that when you are being brave, *you are only battling your own fears;*

your fears of the unknown and your fears of what you feel may happen to you for facing that fear.

Taking that one step further:

The only person who can accurately gauge the courage of a person is *that person alone* and no one else, because only that person knows what he or she had to overcome to do or accomplish something.

Think about any time you had conquered one of your own fears, no matter how small – I'll bet at the time, it didn't seem so small, did it?

People who make comparisons between their opinions of another's bravery are not only slighting the other person, they are slighting themselves. Without even realizing it, they are downplaying their own moments of bravery.

Susan Jeffers said, "Feel the fear and do it anyway." This quote has been repeated so often the real meaning is lost – like so many other important statements (Bible verses included). What fear we feel is personal to each one of us, so how is anyone else able to judge our courage if they don't feel the depth of our fear?

A simple example could be the child who finally stands up to a bully, whether for himself or in defense of another. In the mind of that child, that bully has the power to hurt or kill him. How is that child less brave than a soldier in battle?

It is perspective we need to be able to judge less.

At the very least, we need the perspective that allows us to realize the limits of our own perspective.

I never considered myself to be brave, but I never thought myself to be a coward, either. I like to think that if the time came for me to have courage I would – never paying attention to the full scope of the idea of *doing something that frightens me, ready to face (danger or) pain.*

I know now that I am braver than I used to think. I have consciously began to face my fears and do things in spite of them.

I faced my father when I was 21. You may not think that's a big deal, but my relationship with my father consumed most of my life up until that point (how many times has he been mentioned in these pages?). That wasn't easy for me.

I left an abusive relationship. Some may feel they would never be in one – that is wonderful. But I was. And I got out – two years after I wrote an 'if anything happens to me …' letter. That wasn't easy for me.

I officially announced to anyone within ear- or screen-shot that I was a writer. Small for you, maybe; but not for me. I know how hard it was to feel that I was denying myself a large part of myself for most of my life – I can't imagine how hard it must be for others who've denied more.

I wrote and published about a few bad times in my life. I still feel some measure of fear every time I hit "publish."

Guess what? All of that makes me brave and courageous. How do I know? Because I know how much each one of those steps costs me. Yay me.

Guess what else? *None of it has anything to do with you.* I don't have to explain or make you believe that overcoming any of these issues was brave on my part, nor do I have to take your assessment of how brave my actions have been.

We can only assume the depths of someone else's courage, but we will never know because we are not them. If we can't honestly know how frightened or fearful of some type of pain a person was regarding doing or being something, then we can't honestly know how courageous they were.

Are the people who valiantly 'fight' a battle or disease more courageous than those who aren't fighting anything physical? If so, why? How is that type of selection made? And what about the fact that some people's fear of death is less than their fear of mockery or shame?

There are so many different types of courage; we should not be invalidating any of them by judging only certain forms as valid. We shouldn't be comparing anything. We all have our own obstacles to overcome. *All of us.* And all of us are brave and courageous and heroes when we make the decision to stand up for ourselves to ourselves, without letting the fear of what others may do to us in any way.

Facing up to your fears and standing up for yourself is the basis of being true to our own beliefs. I have mine; you have yours. I am allowed mine just as much as you are allowed yours.

I'm not asking you to change what you believe. I'm just suggesting that you try looking at things from a different perspective – not to change your mind, but to open it enough to give the hate room to escape; to understand that the hate and intolerance you carry for others festers inside of you and robs from you even more than the people your force it on.

If you feel that someone else's actions or efforts are heroic or brave, celebrate it and be inspired by it. If others feel that a person shows courage, and you don't agree, keep it to yourself. By demeaning what someone else feels is somehow worthy, you are taking away something that could inspire them in some way.

We are all in this together, and we waste so much time judging, hating and blaming others, and drawing lines between us that shouldn't be there, instead of celebrating the hero each one of us can be.

Be your own hero by being brave enough to be yourself.

Be more courageous by allowing others to be who they are.

16 WHERE IS THE LOVE

I remember reading a comment that a friend of mine made on social media regarding the parents of a transgender child. His comment regarding this family who is loving their young child in the best way they see fit was, "How disgusting. An abomination to God."

That makes me sad for so many reasons. The first is because those are uncharitable, ugly words of hate and judgment; the second is because those ugly words are cast on a family doing what they feel is best *out of love for their child.* Even if you disagree and think they are grossly misguided, you cannot fault the point of view they are coming from. Nor do you have the right to cast stones. None of us have that right, do we? "Let those without sin cast the first stone." Right? Sin is sin, and whatever your definition of sin is, *you* are still a sinner--and so am I--and you still expect people to love you and treat you with respect, yet you *choose* not to treat others the same way. What happened to the rule of treating others as you would have them treat you? Try to look at it this way: we all sin; some of us just do it *differently*. Besides, weren't we taught not to worry about the splinter in someone else's eye?

The terrorists who attack our country do so out of their religious beliefs. We get angry at them for attacking 'us' (in the only circumstance we consider us all one unit), yet aren't we doing the same to others in our religious judgment of them? No, we may not be physically killing people, but we *are* persecuting them, attempting to kill their choices, their freedoms, their spirits (which is ultimately the same thing). And then we deny that you are doing the same thing the terrorists are doing. And in more irony, their reasoning is the same as ours: 'for their God.' And we find that unacceptable.

Some religions teach that every person before they die will have had the opportunity to hear the *true* Word of the God and that some may make the choice not to follow it and perish for it, even though that loving God has *allowed* every single person to make their own choices.

Many of us have been taught to live by the example Jesus had set - Jesus, who befriended the outcasts and the dregs of society, treating all of them with love; Jesus, who did not attack, spit on, curse, or defame in any way that man who betrayed him directly. If the man we were taught to emulate did not judge and persecute people then, why do we feel the need to do it now, in His name? Are we not putting yourself above him by doing so?

One Mother's Day a woman decided to celebrate by standing out in a busy intersection holding a sign that said, "Thank Your Mom

Today For Not Being Gay" and was assaulted by another woman who threw a drink at her.

Technically speaking, her sign was incorrect; many people have mothers who are not their birth mothers through adoption, which means their mothers *could* be gay--but that's another tangent.

I do not condone the actions of the woman who threw the drink at her; hate as an answer to hate is never effective. What bothered me is that the woman with the sign told reporters she was doing it "out of love."

Public judgment – shaming - never comes from a place of love. Isn't love supposed to be kind?

Isn't everything supposed to be about love? What about 1st Corinthians 13?

> 1 Corinthians 13 - New International Version (NIV)
> "If I speak in the tongues of men or of angels, but do not have love, I am only a resounding gong or a clanging cymbal. If I have the gift of prophecy and can fathom all mysteries and all knowledge, and if I have a faith that can move mountains, but do not have love, I am nothing. If I give all I possess to the poor and give over my body to hardship that I may boast, but do not have love, I gain nothing.
> Love is patient, love is kind. It does not envy, it does not boast, it is not proud. It does not dishonor others, it is not self-seeking, it is not easily angered, it keeps no record of wrongs. Love does not delight in evil but

rejoices with the truth. It always protects, always trusts, always hopes, always perseveres.

Love never fails. But where there are prophecies, they will cease; where there are tongues, they will be stilled; where there is knowledge, it will pass away. For we know in part and we prophesy in part, but when completeness comes, what is in part disappears. When I was a child, I talked like a child, I thought like a child, I reasoned like a child. When I became a man, I put the ways of childhood behind me. For now we see only a reflection as in a mirror; then we shall see face to face. Now I know in part; then I shall know fully, even as I am fully known.

And now these three remain: faith, hope and love. But the greatest of these is love.

Where is the love in persecution? Where is the love in dishonoring others? In keeping record of wrongs? In the lack of tolerance? In not treating others with kindness? In not allowing others the same freedom of choice that your own God gave them?

I have another point to consider: what if the people with different beliefs and lifestyles were put here to test *us* and our own faith? Job was tested. Did he lash out at others? The same bibles that talk about love talk about Job. He suffered immense personal loss - as in, *directly affecting him* - and he attacked no one. Yet some of us feel obligated to persecute people that have no direct effect on our lives other than the fact that they live differently? God made them, too; and God doesn't make mistakes, right?

And 'those people', as they have been called, treat people with more love and tolerance than are shown to them. Think about it. Some people are quite vocal about their judgment of people the moment the words 'alternative lifestyle' is mentioned. I have yet to see a gay person go off on a public tirade about how wrong or 'gross' heterosexuals are when they see pictures of them. Some people regularly post bible verses on social media. And people leave those posts alone, don't they? I've never seen anyone's post of a bible verse attacked by an atheist or homosexual. Why is it that the ones who are being attacked can show more of a 'Christian' attitude of tolerance, love and kindness?

Where is your love? Where is your kindness?

How about this radical idea: why not practice the "Random Act of Kindness" towards someone living a lifestyle you don't agree with? *Unconditional kindness*. The Christian way. Wouldn't that be quite a testament to your faith?

As far as religion goes I will say this: for those that truly believe that their God will have Judgment Day on certain people, then kindly step off and let him do it. If he's going to take care of the people living 'wrong', you have nothing to worry about. Go on with your lives, living them as you see fit, and spend more time worrying about the child molester that just moved into your neighborhood, or the terrorist who is planning to kill all the people who don't believe in the God he or she believes in – which, might not be yours or mine, or the man in your church who everyone loves that goes home and beats his wife and/or children - and the odds are that child-molester, wife-beater and/or terrorist, have been brought up in your so-called 'correct' heterosexual household. These are the people that can harm you.

The silly Gay Marriage debate is all about discrimination, and discrimination only. Slavery, racial discrimination, gender discrimination... we've seen this same fight countless times before. It's about some people arguing the *completely personal* freedoms that are afforded all of us in the Bill of Rights:

"That government is instituted, and ought to be exercised for the benefit of the people; which consists in the enjoyment of life and liberty, with the right of acquiring and using property, and generally of pursuing and obtaining happiness and safety."

At first I thought "Gay Marriage" was about a themed wedding. Disco Balls, dancing, lots of glitter and fabulous outfits. I was *so* disappointed when I realized all this fuss was just about regular marriage.

The two people that only want to love each other and stand together equally with everyone else will not interfere with the happiness or safety of others.

I count myself lucky to be born after all the wonderful women and men who fought for women's rights. The only discrimination I've faced is in the left-over chauvinism, and even that has lessened over the course of my life. Yet even that can get to me. I can't imagine being treated with the direct discrimination some people still have to deal with on a daily basis based on simply who they are or who they love.

Love. Isn't that what it's supposed to be all about? When people are loving towards each other there is less fighting. Want to raise hell for a cause? Fight hatred.

A lot of the argument on marriage equality has to do with using the money and benefits of *traditional* marriage as another means of exclusion. As if a marriage between two women or two men will affect the marriage rights of a man and woman. If you want to argue the money, keep in mind that no job is allowed to discriminate, either. A qualified person is a qualified person and should get equality there. The similarities on paper between and job and a marriage contract are enough that, technically speaking, this ridiculous argument should have been settled with job equality.

And, speaking of ridiculous, we are not there yet either, are we?

One other thing, most of my gay and trans friends are in healthier and longer-lasting relationships than most of my family (myself included), and some of my straight friends are only *still* married because it's too expensive to get a divorce. And judging by the divorce rate and spousal killings alone, it looks like we 'straight' people don't have it right, either.

Supposedly we are closest to knowing God when we are choosing our highest thought; therefore, God cannot be as judgmental as some say, because choosing judgment is not choosing the highest thought.

Sometimes judgment of others is the reaction to the envy we feel when we see someone free of the limits we've allowed others to impose on us.

We need to allow love in all forms without judging it.

17 LOOKING FOR LOVE

I was doing research (getting lost on the internet) when I saw the title, "3 Things That Repel Men" and clicked on the link. I wanted to make sure I was doing it right. What I heard was a 15 minute sales pitch from a woman promising to sell her secret on how to get a man. After five minutes I was appalled, after 10 minutes I was humiliated and hurt, and after the full fifteen I was offended and outraged - for myself, for women, and then for all of us.

This is how she started:

> "I am so-and-so, and in a few minutes I am to show you how to break through even the toughest guy's shell... Reach deep into his heart and have him begging you to be with him forever! Watch this short video to the end and discover how I stumbled on a simple secret that ignites his passion for you, and has him bending over backwards to please you... Adore you...And honestly give you everything you could possibly

want... Without playing games! It's so simple it's embarrassing... And yet I insist that I can quickly teach the simple secret to you... Instantly giving you the power in your relationship."

There are so many things wrong with what she says right there alone. And she got worse.

For the record, this is for all of us, not just the women. I may focus more on women...well, because I am one. Women have been dealing with shit like this forever. Movies, magazines, music, etc. But certain things are finally being discussed and dealt with. Photoshop. That one word brings up the new awareness of what magazines have done and still are doing to women. Women in movies - not just actresses - are realizing the importance of the effect they have on women. (This actually goes to all groups that are stereotyped or put in a certain 'place' in the media - another example of all the lines drawn between us). But the reason I took special exception to this...spiel, is because this woman is trying to sell this line of bullshit to other women. One of our own has turned on us and trying to profit from it. She starts off by saying "No games" then outlines a *strategy*. If that is not turning it into a game, I don't know what is.

She even went so far as to say something along the lines of "(women have said)...that girl isn't half as good as I am, yet she found someone and I'm stuck with the losers." I thought we stopped saying that in high school.

This is not just a problem with women. Both men and women have been dealing with loneliness and emptiness and feelings of 'incomplete-ness' simply because they were taught by their environment that they weren't enough on their own.

What this woman is selling...not for $99.00...not for $69.00...but a *one time* payment of $39.00...

is that there is something wrong with you.

> "But wait! If you act now (and you have to, because the price is going to go back up if you don't order by midnight—Hey, I've already charged thousands of dollars to women for this secret [don't worry; they can afford it] and it's not fair to them that I drop the price so drastically just to get the word out), I will *give* you another book that the title of basically repeats what I said I was going to give you in the initial package!"

> "*And*, if you purchase this I will add *another* book with a title that suggests I left something out of the first book that I promised to tell you!"

(On a side note, I wonder when people will stop falling for this kind of advertising.)

But here's where she really crosses the line:

> "This system will work for anyone! *Even if...*"

(Are you all ready for this?)

> "You are a few pounds overweight."

(I will *not* abbreviate this) *What the fuck?*

> "Even if..."

(If the previous comment wasn't enough to make you throw up a little in your mouth. Or cry.)

"You have children."

- *Wait! What?*

What is wrong with us? That is not a question, it's more of an accusation. What is the deal about the focus we put on 'Relationships'? Why does a romantic relationship merit more attention than other relationships? And what does our weight or parental status have to do with our ability to connect with another person?

Isn't everything that we are involved in some sort of relationship? We have a relationship with our job, our self-image, even money. We have relationships with family, friends, and pets. The idea of a Romantic Relationship for some reason appears to take precedence over all of them, including what should be the most important relationship we have: the one we have with our own self.

Before I go further and offend anyone with this, let me state that when I am talking about 'people' I am talking in very general terms. Before any single - someone who is not in a Romantic Relationship - person gets offended, know that I am not talking about *you* specifically. I am aware that there are people who are in well-adjusted relationships as well as those that are single and quite happy (and I'm happy for all of you), but there are still many people who will fall for this *special* $39.00 *deal*. And I say that backed by what we are bombarded with in our daily lives, like the myth of marriage equaling happily-ever-after and the idea of single people being social outcasts to couples, or that the only way anyone can be *truly* loved is by having someone to celebrate Valentine's Day with or someone to kiss on New Year's Eve. Why have we been taught at a young age to look for that kind of relationship? To feel that without them we are nothing? Why are we led to believe that our lives are incomplete without one? That line from the Jerry Maguire, the one that is considered oh-so-romantic, "You complete me." is bullshit. When do we realize that we do not need anyone to 'complete' us? We are complete; we are already perfect …already loved. We *are* love.

To be happy is to find happiness within ourselves. In The Wizard of Oz the tin woodsman asked, "What have you learned, Dorothy?" And Dorothy answered, "Well, if I ever go looking for my heart's desire again, I won't look any further than my own backyard. Because if it isn't there, I never really lost it to begin with!" Confucius said, "Happiness consists not in having what you want, but in wanting what you have." This is not new information for anyone, yet so many of us are still running around looking for things to make us happy - looking for *people* to make us happy. Why is that? What is wrong with us? Who told us that there was something missing? Part of me thinks sometimes it's just a skewed version of the idea behind the thought that we are all connected. That people think that it's a literal connection that we need to make with people. That we are like random puzzle pieces on the kitchen table, sorted into groups of similar color, shape, and whether or not we have 'straight' edges (yes, that was very tongue-in-cheek) waiting to be paired with that one piece that fits us perfectly. We are not connected like that. We are not made to be connected like that. We are connected by the simple fact that we're human, each one of us is made like the other with the same essence. What is inside, our organs, our blood, our body structure, are the same. Our spirits are of the same energy; the connections we notice that we have with others can have different depths and strengths, and that has to do with the levels we are connecting with them on—how their energies 'match' ours. Our differences are only on the outside, and they are few. I am you and you are me. And still, people have to draw lines between each other based on gender, religion, color, ethnicity, sexual orientation, and anything that a collective group of people perceive to be "different", even if those differences are differences we are born with.

And after drawing all those lines and sorting our differences between each other, we go back and look for our connections? That doesn't make sense.

What makes even less sense is spending money to let someone tell us how incomplete we are without a Romantic Relationship.

I've had the same best friend since we were 7 years old, and this friendship has outlasted both of our marriages (yes, plural). I also have many other friends that have been around since middle school, high school, most of my jobs, both of my marriages – you get the picture.

As I got older, and had more bad - not always bad, but not lasting - Romantic Relationships I began to fully appreciate the importance of having friends. True friends. And then I started questioning why romantic relationships can be so much work, when a true friendship is really effortless. Did you ever realize that you can say absolutely anything – anything - to a true friend? Think about this. You can say whatever you want to them, and they can do the same to you—and you will still be friends. This obviously is the biggest indicator that you should be true friends with your romantic interest. My friends (and I am so lucky to have the circle around me that I do) love me, support me, encourage me, kick me in the ass when I need it, cry with me, laugh with me, and most of all allow me to be me. There is an incredible freedom in that alone; to be able to just be and know that you are loved no matter what. The only thing I don't do with my friends is have sex with them.

So, why then aren't friendships held so highly? Or, rather, why are they given a back seat to that other kind of relationship (you know, the ones you do have sex in)? Or, why don't we have that same freedom in the love/sex relationships? Why is it that we can just be ourselves with our friends but we have to be something else to or with a 'love interest'? We are not supposed to be who we are because we are now someone's significant other? Are we in those relationships merely to reflect an image for them? Why are there 'rules'? Or strategies?

Let's go back to Confucius on the yellow brick road: we have everything we need inside us to make us happy. There is no reason to *look* for anything to do it for us. We grow up being taught that in so many ways. "Money can't buy happiness," right? If you are never happy with what you have, you will never be happy with what you get. By that same token, if you are never happy with who you are, you will never be happy with who you are with. You have to be happy with what you have and with who you are before you will ever be able to enjoy anything or anyone else. This is the essential secret behind real friendships (and I mean the *real* ones): there are no expectations for them to be anything other than who they are. We don't expect our friends to take care of us or fix us, and they don't expect us to fix them. We just want to spend time with them and enjoy being ourselves while they are being themselves. We don't look for anything more, because nothing more is needed. If you think about that, and if you have those kinds of friends, then what more do you need? Why do you have to go out and look for anything else when you have unconditional love right there? Seriously, if it's just sex that's missing, it is easy enough to get without compromising yourself just to get it.

When we go out looking for something or someone, we are operating under the impression that something is missing. We are coming from that place of lack. If lack is the focus, lack is more of what we will get. How many times have we realized that the best things that have happened to us happened unexpectedly? When we weren't looking or trying for it? Even in the simple example of when you lose your keys, or are trying to remember something: When do you find the keys? When do you remember 'that thing'? When you have relaxed and stopped stressing about it. That is the answer. Relax. Stop stressing about it. It will come to you.

Relax. Stop stressing. Be happy (yes, it is a choice). Be you. Everything else will come to you. Don't expect anyone to take care of you, to fix you, to make you happy. And don't go looking for someone to take care of, to fix, or to make happy. We all should learn to be happy first with ourselves, then we are able to just 'play' with others, and enjoy each other. Like we do and are with our friends.

If you do go looking for *Someone*, make sure it's just because you are ready to share yourself and not to look for any kind of completion. Please, please, *please*, realize first how wonderful you truly are. Be aware of everything that you and only you can offer to share with someone else. Do not try to buy them, or take care of them, or by trying to ingratiate yourself into their space and forcing them see how much they 'need' you. You are not and cannot be responsible for someone else's happiness, and you should never dare to expect that of or put that level of responsibility on anyone else. That alone adds pressure to a relationship that should never be there.

Think of it in terms of goals; once we achieve a goal, we move on to the next. If you feel you need to feel needed, once a need is fulfilled you will want to look for something else. Needing to have someone love you *in that way* will only be satisfied for a little while, because once that need is fulfilled you will upgrade the goal to include preference. It goes from, "I want someone to love me" to "I want someone to love me who is or does [this]." This is why we can't enter into Romantic Relationships that are need-based.

I am telling you right now that you are fucking perfect the way you are, and you already have and are everything you need. It does not matter how you got here. Please, know this much. Find your happiness inside and then you will see it outside. It was never missing and it never left.

Stop drawing lines between people, between groups. Be yourself. Then you will notice that the people that are around you are the ones that appreciate who and what you are. No games, no strategies. Then you can enjoy each other with no expectations for anything other than just that.

And if you read this far and still don't agree with me, you can at least be happy that I said something nice about you. For free.

But if you'd like to pay money to be told that you are a fucking moron who will be alone and lonely forever, email me. I'm sure we can work something out.

18 A DUCK, OR TOO GOOD TO BE TRUE?

Is there really such a thing as being "too good to be true"? If it looks like a duck and acts like a duck, isn't it a duck? Why is it only a duck sometimes, when other times it can look like a duck and act like a duck, and instead of being a duck it's too good to be true?

We've all experienced the concept one way or another. We have imagined fantastical experiences like winning billions of dollars in the lottery, or surpassing Marilyn Monroe's icon status. We discount these flights of fancy as 'too good to be true' because we have no belief in the possibility of these events ever coming to be. Closer to home, in our 'real' lives, we've had experiences arise of circumstances like a surprise job opportunity, a new relationship, or a new situation where it seemed - however momentarily - that the stars have aligned in our favor. *For once*. With the adage, "If it seems too good to be true, it usually is." ringing in our ears, along with our faith in that sentiment, we may actually and turn our backs on those opportunities of new life situations. Why bother? It never would have worked out because it was too good to be true.

That 'why bother' attitude limits you more than you know. It interferes with your belief in possibility, including any possibility of improvement, and prevents you from really trying to achieve a goal or get what you want, because you will only try to do something or attain something if you truly believe it is possible.

But what if there was no such possibility of anything being too good to be true? Good is a relative term and it depends on perspective. What may be considered good by one person may not be good for another. Not only that, good is only noticeable because of the existence of that which we perceive to be bad. Imagine the different turns our lives may have taken if we accepted new situations or new experiences without that judgment of being 'too good'. And what if by not condemning them as unreal they really did evolve into what we glimpsed as a potential reality?

What if, in fact, the only reason we condemned something as being too good to be true is because of fear? That maybe, no matter how open we perceive our minds to be, in our efforts to protect ourselves from being hurt or disappointed (which is what all of the reasons basically boil down to) we have actually closed a part of our minds off to the ability to believe in what is possible?

If something seems too good to be true, it usually is.

Right - but not because the situation isn't good or can't be good, but because you don't trust it to be good.

How many times have you heard yourself say that you don't trust something?

Do you realize what you are doing? When you say that you don't trust, you are showing *total trust* - just in something else; usually, the opposite of the situation as it appears and in its possibilities. It's not that you are not trusting the situation or circumstance; you are trusting your disbelief in it.

To deem something as too good to be true is to say that nothing good is true or lasting, and this is why you find that you've settled for low-hanging fruit – even though you have the ability to be aware of the pride you can have in yourself when you've achieved a goal despite supposed odds. You are giving prior judgment to a situation as negative, despite its positive appearance. Why?

Why can't we believe all the time that something is exactly what it appears to be? People use the phrase "Seeing is believing" all the time, yet will not always believe what they see. What makes them so selective?

Fear.

Will believing in something we can see make us vulnerable to it? How? We see many things every time we open our eyes, and we aren't afraid of them. Just certain things?

If you feel you are vulnerable to something, recognize that there is a special power in being vulnerable, because vulnerability is really an openness to possibility. It puts you in a position of gaining something that you would never attain by 'playing it safe'. There are no possibilities without giving something a shot.

There are people that hide from honest relationships because they don't want to be vulnerable to someone else – forgetting that the other person will be vulnerable, too.

Vulnerability is trust. Trust is belief. Belief is always positive. If the thought of vulnerability causes fear, there is a predetermined judgment of the situation as being negative, even if all indications of it point otherwise. Vulnerability is really an openness to possibility, to believe that anything can happen – even good things.

So, it looks good (looks like a duck), feels good (acts like a duck), but you don't believe it's good (it's a duck), and because of that you won't let it be good (a duck)?

That poor duck.

Once you've labeled something as too good to be true, you have already condemned it to being so. The statement itself will become a self-fulfilling prophecy.

When you trust in something, all of your actions around it are positive and integrative; when you don't trust in it, your actions are negative and segregative. Basically, even if you have made the decision to go along with something, any distrust you have will cause you to withhold yourself from honest immersion in it. You can't give anything your all if your all isn't present, and the situation is doomed before it starts.

(But you already knew that, didn't you?)

Believing in something can never be destructive because it will not interfere with the situation or circumstance and will allow it to flow. Attempting to act on something you don't truly believe in will cause you to react to your mistrust, instead of allowing what you 'hope' will happen.

Remember, the opposite of hope is despair. You don't want to hope, you want to know. Believing and trusting is knowing.

If it looks like a duck and acts like a duck, it's a duck. If it looks good and feels good, it is good.

(And it's true.)

Let the duck be a duck.

Believe in the duck.

Allow it to be a duck.

It will be a duck.

19 COLLECTIVE ENERGY IN MOTION

I talk a lot about all of us being part of a collective and collective energy. The energy and spirit that run through all of us are what unite us despite our differences – those differences being on the surface only, like flavorings. You may prefer lobster and I prefer steak, but eating them produces the same feelings of contentment and satisfaction. The endorphins that the runner enjoys is comparable to the feeling of flying a dancer feels. Our differences highlight our sameness.

The idea of collective consciousness began initially as a part of studies done of transcendental meditation and the 'unified field' consciousness within a group, but has since been picked up as being viably scientific. Studies have not only been done on families, countries and the more common groups but also on the stock market, marketing and trends in consumer behavior. Other variations (and not as much of a stretch as one may think) are peer pressure, the (mistaken) perception and current popular references of lemmings, mass hysteria, and even in the ideas of 'keeping up with the Joneses' and 'misery loves company'. Mob mentality is the term used to define the negative of the herd mentality, the cooperative behavior of groups.

What do all of these have in common? The fact that each group shares a particular belief or set of beliefs that arise out of a shared set of emotions. The emotional base is the energy behind all of these collectives, no matter the size.

There is energy in emotions. The energy that comes from individual people's emotions combine to create a larger field, a collective. The stronger the emotions, the stronger the energy. Scientific data aside (and there is plenty), this can be proven simply by walking in a room where two people were having an argument. They may have immediately stopped when you walked in but you are aware that they were arguing, even if they smiled at you in greeting. Why? What's the common phrase? *The tension was so thick you could cut it with a knife.* That is a direct reference to the energy outside of and created by the two people arguing that is palpably felt by others. Collective consciousness occurs when others around are experiencing emotional energy that matches or has a frequency close to that energy they come into contact with. If the energy matches, they can join together; if the frequencies are close enough, they can be 'persuaded' to follow, and the field gets bigger. If you were already experiencing negative emotions when you walked into the room, theirs would feed yours and you would leave feeling worse. If your energy was positive, you would be able to brush it off without a thought.

In many of the negative cases the emotional base is fear (fear of exclusion, fear of being singled out, fear of being considered different, fear of harm, etc.) and/or greed. Love and happiness are equally strong emotions. But the magnetic attraction of energies happen only when their frequencies match. For comparative purposes, the widely-used opposite ends of the scale are fear and love, with every other emotion being somewhere in between. We either make a decision based on fear (the fear of the repercussions of any other choice, what we perceive to be the lesser of two evils, fear of leaving a comfort zone, etc.) or love (something that we know will make us feel happy).

The so-called lemmings, the people who wish to keep up with the others, those who are accused of being easily swayed or influenced or 'not having their own mind' are still following the pull of their own energies based on their emotional states. This is not to say they are victims or easy prey, so much as they are unaware of their own base beliefs and feelings and of their true ability to control them.

Collective energy has no boundaries. It can be carried and spread across everything, time and space included. Anything that carries emotion is a conduit for energy. Even words. Sometimes, *especially* words. The power of words is carried in the emotions they evoke. The art of persuading people has to do with either being able to tap into their current emotional state or having the ability to raise or lower their emotional frequencies to create a desired belief. You can easily convince a person that a situation is unfair even if he or she has no active part in it if that person is already in the state of feeling unfairly treated by another, unrelated situation.

Think about it. Fighting *the man*. Voting for the underdog. Oppression and subjugation. Family feuds that stretch across generations. Sympathy pains. All—and more—are carried and strengthened by a knowledge and acceptance of the emotions underneath, even by secondary participants.

I often refer to music the 'Universal Leveler'. It brings people together *because of the emotions it evokes*. Music has the ability to resonate with our emotional energies, and can both raise and lower them. We've all seen the many videos on YouTube set to Pharrell's *Happy*. People have separate playlists for romantic dates and working out. How many times have you heard someone say, "This song gets me *pumped!*"? How do you feel when you hear *Amazing Grace*? What about *We're Not Gonna Take It?* What's it like being in a bar and hearing that song? Music is the most obvious proof of collective energy.

Another point about the art of persuasion and emotional energy: mob mentality starts with one person who has negative emotions about a situation (sadly, this could even be just the one person who is never happy who feels better when everyone around is also unhappy, or gets pleasure by taking people down). That person finds someone who feels the same way, and then another. Persuasion comes in when the group is being built deliberately. Here is where peer pressure begins. Mass hysteria comes out of a concerted effort to fan the flames of emotion.

Notice the trends on our media. What happened with ebola, now that vaping is the issue? Did it lose its importance? Two people arguing on the same side, as in complaining about a current situation together, will create a separate collective that can build just by inviting another person of the same opinions as theirs to their cause. Like the old Faberge Organics Shampoo commercial, "and they'll tell two friends, and so on, and so on…"

Verbal persuasion does not rely only on select words, but the tone behind them. The tone sets the emotional base by its relation to a similar emotion in the other person. How the first sentence is spoken can make the difference between a debate and an argument. Constructive criticism or a difference of opinion can be taken as a verbal attack based on the quality of how it is delivered.

What adds to a negative collective is often misunderstanding. This is not exclusive to those who were a part of the origin of the group; in many cases situations get inflamed by someone who joins late who is misinformed, does not have all of the facts or does not understand the whole situation, but because his or her own emotional base matches the general feeling he or she will pick up the torch and set everything around on fire. These people are specific targets of people looking to persuade a larger group, for whatever reason. Lemmings and mass hysteria, anyone?

How does one go about destroying a particular collective? Go after the weakest link; the one whose emotional base isn't as defined as the rest. A marriage isn't ruined by an outsider; there is really no such thing as a home wrecker. If the emotional commitment is equally strong on both sides, there is no thought of temptation. We all know the adage about the grass being greener on the other side.

A happy person cannot be persuaded by anyone to do something they don't want to do; they make choices based on how they feel. One large problem is that not everyone is happy. When you are in a negative place it can feel so very hard to get out of it. And jumping on a bandwagon of other unhappy people for a united cause is a pleasant diversion from facing and dealing with our own unhappiness or unrest. That way, we can outwardly express the emotions we feel and shit all over the place - but on someone else's lawn.

But emotions can be controlled, or at least modified a little at a time. Smiles are contagious, tears can be contagious. Tension and anger are also contagious, even if the causes are different. But it's the emotions that determine participation in anything.

Why don't night owls and morning people view 5 a.m. the same way? Why do I want to hurl a snowball at my lovely friend, Tina, who expresses joy at every snowflake that falls?

The emotions around the events are different. They will not combine.

Collectives are wonderful when they spread positivity, and destructive when not. Isn't it better to use our energies on building rather than breaking down? Re-building can take a lot more energy and sometimes more time than we have. Wouldn't we rather use our powers for good?

Before we react or join in any collective - we are not drawn in or persuaded to join; we are invited and we have a choice in whether or not to accept that invitation - that is in any way incendiary we need to make sure that our emotional involvement is tied to a full understanding to avoid things being destructively blown out of proportion. And sometimes, even if we have a small opinion about an event, we need to let it be fought out by the actual participants and stay out of it (unless, of course, it is your intent to control a desired outcome).

We all need to pay attention to where we put our energy, and whether or not we are concerned with construction or destruction. We need to understand how and why we feel a certain way about anything, and what emotions underline our opinions. Whether or not our scales are tipped towards fear or love.

If we have been a part of something destructive (it doesn't matter the size of the role we played), we need to take a step back and re-examine the situation and see if we want to re-build.

If the choice is to give up, examine why you feel that way, too, with the understanding of which way your scale is tipping. Keep in mind, leaving a situation for dead will leave a sour taste in your mouth that you will savor at every thought of it. That energy will carry on (and so on, and so on, and so on...). Who knows where else you will be influenced by it.

On the bright side, even after destruction can come a stronger rebirth, a stronger unity. As long as we breathe there is hope, right? Just as negative energy can bring us down, positive energy can raise us up. Even if you look at that selfishly, if all you care about is how *you* feel, it is still in your own best interest to put your energy on the collective side of positivity, so that that energy keeps coming back to you.

We can rebuild. Always.

Today is a new day; now is a new moment.

I hope you feel good about that.

20 ONE VOICE

Just as there are no new ideas, nothing presented here is anything new. So why speak out? Why put myself out there? There are many reasons why there is a use for more than one voice. Think of your favorite song. The song is broken down by music and lyrics; the music is broken down by instrumentation with each instrument playing its own sound and the lyrics are sung in another voice, or more than one at the same time. Harmonic together, they produce the melody that resonates with you.

Has there ever been a song you disliked until another artist remade it? A different musician or singer puts his or her own spin on it - a song you already know - and all of a sudden it becomes something you are willing to listen to. Like the stereotypical teenage child who ignores the advice of parents yet will 'hear' that same advice given by a friend, sometimes it's the delivery - or the messenger - of a thought that can influence whether or not it's heard.

People speak different languages; a translator is needed, not to say something different but to say the same thing in a different way so that it might be understood.

But these are just justifications to back up the real reason: why does anyone feel compelled to do anything? Why does anyone feel passionate about something?

It's all about expression. The fact that in each different expression we can find some base similarities that reinforce our connections. I read a lot, and I listen to audiobooks. Sometimes I'm surprised to hear someone saying the same thing that I've been saying for a while. Sometimes I hear something that resonates with me, something that I want to write about. When I sit down to write, do I let the fact that other people might be saying the same thing stop me from writing about it? I'll be honest, I've had my own moments of question. He said it better than I can. She is a person that people will listen to; why will they listen to me or read something that I wrote? If I'm basically saying the same things they are, why say it?

We all have our preferences; usually if we prefer a subject or specific type of storyline we tend to read others like it and we find value in all of them – even if the only value is to show us which type we like better. Sometimes we understand ourselves better with each new voice we hear.

Sometimes, it is just a matter of enjoying a particular storyline, type of comedy, music, art medium or theme as entertainment, and we listen to every variation.

Even one voice sings many different notes. When you hear a musical artist you enjoy, do you limit yourself to listening to only one of their songs?

I am simply adding my voice to a collective. So what if I'm singing the same song? I have my own spin, my own sound, and I'm fully aware that even discord can help create a beautiful harmony.

I believe in the idea of a collective and in its power. When we don't think for ourselves and are unhappy with the world we live in, it's easy to miss the fact that we are one of the bricks in the wall that we keep banging our heads against. The methods we use to isolate and exclude other people around us conversely manage to isolate and exclude us from them.

Once we feel isolated on our own, we feel a sort of reverse arrogance in that good things happen only to other people, other people can change, other people can break through their demons, but the lowly 'I' can't; then isolation and loneliness become self-imposed.

A funny thing is that even in self-imposed exile you cannot separate yourself from others. You may be staying home alone on a Saturday night, but you are not the only one staying home alone on a Saturday night.

I am one of those people who isn't completely satisfied with all that is around me. I even complain about things. But there's one rule I have for myself about complaining: If I'm not willing to work to change something I have no right to complain about it.

I do want to change what's around me and change has to start somewhere. I keep a quote by Elie Wiesel nearby that strongly resonates with me:

> *"But where was I to start? The world is so vast, I shall start with the country I knew best, my own. But my country is so very large. I had better start with my town. But my town, too, is large. I had best start with my street. No, my home. No, my family. Never mind, I shall start with myself."*

Starting with myself begins with knowing myself, my preferences and why I think the way I do. When I find something I don't like about me I try to get control of it so that I can like myself more. That like turns to love, and once I have that I can spread it around. Then I stand proudly as who I am, and then I connect with other like-minded people. When our voices join we become a powerful energy.

When one person stands, others stand with her. In Massachusetts in 2014, employees of a popular chain of grocery stores rallied together – not for more money or benefits, but to maintain a management that they felt benefitted the people and not the corporate board, and they succeeded. Governments and monarchies can be overthrown by the people banding together in unity. Sitting around commiserating over beer doesn't count; your voices may get louder, but you won't be very effective in creating the change you want to see.

Sometimes it is fear that keeps people quiet; fear of being seen, fear of reprisal, and fear of failure. But nobody truly knows how effective they can be until they try, and they will never know the people that feel the same way they do until they stand up an speak.

Hearing someone else say what you feel can remind you that you are not alone – this is what makes songs resonate with so many people at once. They underline our connectedness with each other and help us feel not so isolated.

Like Barry Manilow sang, "All it takes is one voice, and everyone will sing."

The brick on its own may be strong, but it takes many bricks to build a wall – a wall to keep people in *and* out; it takes more than one individual's thoughts to challenge a long-standing, widely-held belief or idea.

It's said that a chain is only as strong as its weakest link. You may think you are a weak link, or not as effective as someone else, but the flip side of that saying is that the weakest link is the strongest because it's the make or break point of the chain.

The best part about all of this is that you don't have to try and do or be anything to have an impact on those around you to get them to sing with you. Your impact is already created by your existence, so all you have to worry about is knowing who you are so that you can be who you are. Your vibe attracts your tribe. Nobody leaves this world without leaving a footprint. You don't create impact; you reveal it.

Be yourself. Be proud of who you are. Open your mouth and sing – you might be surprised at who starts to sing with you. Create your happy reality by knowing that you have control of how you swing at the balls life throws at you.

Or don't.

I'm not trying to cause a revolution; change is constant. I know I'm just an echo of many other voices and this is how I express myself.

With just words.

ABOUT THE AUTHOR

Sue Roulusonis is a single mother of two who, with no formal education, training, or trust fund has managed to accomplish reaching the age of 52 through trial and error and enough bad decisions to complete a set. Edgy to those who like her and a pain in the ass to those who don't, she throws her words out regularly and deliberately with the understanding that even shock value has a time and a place, however inappropriate. She lives in Massachusetts with her younger child who is not yet old enough to escape and two cats who stay because she feeds them.